Ancient Assyria: A Very Short Introduction

VERY SHORT INTRODUCTIONS are for anyone wanting a stimulating and accessible way into a new subject. They are written by experts, and have been translated into more than 40 different languages.

The series began in 1995, and now covers a wide variety of topics in every discipline. The VSI library now contains over 350 volumes—a Very Short Introduction to everything from Psychology and Philosophy of Science to American History and Relativity—and continues to grow in every subject area.

Very Short Introductions available now:

ACCOUNTING Christopher Nobes
ADVERTISING Winston Fletcher
AFRICAN AMERICAN RELIGION
    Eddie S. Glaude Jr.
AFRICAN HISTORY John Parker and
    Richard Rathbone
AFRICAN RELIGIONS
    Jacob K. Olupona
AGNOSTICISM Robin Le Poidevin
ALEXANDER THE GREAT
    Hugh Bowden
AMERICAN HISTORY Paul S. Boyer
AMERICAN IMMIGRATION
    David A. Gerber
AMERICAN LEGAL HISTORY
    G. Edward White
AMERICAN POLITICAL HISTORY
    Donald Critchlow
AMERICAN POLITICAL PARTIES
    AND ELECTIONS L. Sandy Maisel
AMERICAN POLITICS Richard M. Valelly
THE AMERICAN PRESIDENCY
    Charles O. Jones
AMERICAN SLAVERY
    Heather Andrea Williams
THE AMERICAN WEST Stephen Aron
AMERICAN WOMEN'S HISTORY
    Susan Ware
ANAESTHESIA Aidan O'Donnell
ANARCHISM Colin Ward
ANCIENT ASSYRIA Karen Radner
ANCIENT EGYPT Ian Shaw
ANCIENT EGYPTIAN ART AND
    ARCHITECTURE Christina Riggs
ANCIENT GREECE Paul Cartledge

THE ANCIENT NEAR EAST
    Amanda H. Podany
ANCIENT PHILOSOPHY Julia Annas
ANCIENT WARFARE Harry Sidebottom
ANGELS David Albert Jones
ANGLICANISM Mark Chapman
THE ANGLO-SAXON AGE John Blair
THE ANIMAL KINGDOM
    Peter Holland
ANIMAL RIGHTS David DeGrazia
THE ANTARCTIC Klaus Dodds
ANTISEMITISM Steven Beller
ANXIETY Daniel Freeman and
    Jason Freeman
THE APOCRYPHAL GOSPELS
    Paul Foster
ARCHAEOLOGY Paul Bahn
ARCHITECTURE Andrew Ballantyne
ARISTOCRACY William Doyle
ARISTOTLE Jonathan Barnes
ART HISTORY Dana Arnold
ART THEORY Cynthia Freeland
ASTROBIOLOGY David C. Catling
ATHEISM Julian Baggini
AUGUSTINE Henry Chadwick
AUSTRALIA Kenneth Morgan
AUTISM Uta Frith
THE AVANT GARDE David Cottington
THE AZTECS Davíd Carrasco
BACTERIA Sebastian G. B. Amyes
BARTHES Jonathan Culler
THE BEATS David Sterritt
BEAUTY Roger Scruton
BESTSELLERS John Sutherland
THE BIBLE John Riches

For more information visit our website

www.oup.com/vsi/

Karen Radner

ANCIENT ASSYRIA

A Very Short Introduction

OXFORD
UNIVERSITY PRESS

OXFORD
UNIVERSITY PRESS

Great Clarendon Street, Oxford, OX2 6DP,
United Kingdom

Oxford University Press is a department of the University of Oxford.
It furthers the University's objective of excellence in research, scholarship,
and education by publishing worldwide. Oxford is a registered trade mark of
Oxford University Press in the UK and in certain other countries

© Karen Radner 2015

The moral rights of the author have been asserted

First edition published in 2015

Published in the United States of America by Oxford University Press
198 Madison Avenue, New York, NY 10016, United States of America

British Library Cataloguing in Publication Data
Data available

Library of Congress Control Number: 2014951320

ISBN 978-0-19-871590-0

Printed and bound by
CPI Group (UK) Ltd, Croydon, CR0 4YY

To Amélie, with love and admiration

Contents

Acknowledgements

I wish to thank Luciana O'Flaherty, Andrea Keegan, Jenny Nugee, Emma Ma, and Carrie Hickman at OUP who oversaw the book's genesis from conception to completion as well as the anonymous expert and editorial readers who commented astutely and encouragingly on the proposal and the manuscript. I am indebted to Hartmut Kühne, Julian Reade, and Michael Roaf for their kind permission to reproduce, respectively, two images of the Tell Sheikh Hamad Project, an original drawing and a site plan, and to Alessio Palmisano for creating the map at short notice.

Frans van Koppen and Erika Radner read the first complete draft of the book, with Dieter Radner providing some key suggestions for Chapter 1, while Amélie Kuhrt read the final manuscript. I am very grateful for their suggestions and continual support. My thanks extend to Paul, Dibbes, and Mita for their energizing and calming influence on my study's atmosphere.

List of illustrations

Chapter 1
Introducing Assyria

Ancient Assyria is just one of many states flourishing in the
Middle East in the millennia before the beginning of the common
era, but the long-lived kingdom was certainly one of the most
influential. Looking back at an eventful history already spanning
over a millennium, this state emerged in the 9th century BC as the
first world empire. Decisions made in the imperial capital cities
in present day northern Iraq influenced lives from the Nile to the
Caspian Sea while its political, administrative, and infrastructural
heritage profoundly shaped the subsequent history of the wider
Mediterranean region and the Middle East.

Assyrian culture is at once familiar and strange. We may share
the Assyrian taste for good wines, but perhaps would not choose
locusts on a stick for nibbles. A fresh water supply, indoor toilets,
and a well-functioning sewage system in the family home are as
important to us as to urban Assyrians, but we may find it less
essential to have an underground burial chamber accessible from
the living room. We may congratulate Assyrian buyers on enjoying
consumer protection and extended warranties, but are perhaps
taken aback to find that these extended to the purchase of people
who were subject to a 100-day guarantee against epilepsy and
mental instability. The foldable parasol was a practical Assyrian
invention, but carrying one was dangerous: its use was exclusively

reserved for royalty and without entitlement was an act of treason. We, too, enclose letters in envelopes, but they are not made out of clay.

Since the archaeological rediscovery of Assyria in the mid-19th century, its cities have been excavated extensively in Iraq, Syria, Turkey, and Israel, with further sites in Iran, Lebanon, and Jordan providing important information. It is because of the fact that durable clay was the Assyrians' most common writing material that we know so much about these idiosyncrasies and many other details of their culture.

The city-state of Aššur

Assyrian history begins in the city of Aššur which was founded early in the third millennium BC, most likely as a trading emporium to supply the Sumerian cities in the south of modern Iraq with merchandise from the north. From the mid-third millennium BC onwards, textual sources document how the city was periodically integrated into large states centred in the south. The city was part of the realms of the kings of Akkad, then under a local ruler, and later of the kings of Ur. During the latters' time, a career official was dispatched from the south to govern the city: Zarriqum later rose to an even more prestigious post as the regent of Elam in Iran.

After the disintegration of the Ur kingdom around 2000 BC, Aššur was again an independent city-state. Its inhabitants spoke Assyrian. It is a Semitic language, like modern Arabic and Hebrew. Assyrian is a distinct language, albeit closely related to Babylonian, which was used in the regions south of Aššur. In antiquity, only the latter was called 'Akkadian', although today both Assyrian and Babylonian are often described as Akkadian dialects. The cuneiform script was used to record both languages, but the respective signs look quite different and are easily distinguished by experts.

After independence, hereditary local rulers once again governed the city, but they did not style themselves as kings, as the overlords from Akkad and Ur had done. Instead, they asserted that 'Aššur is king and Silulu is representative of Aššur', as one ruler's inscription of the early second millennium BC puts it. The city's god, who shared its name and was the divine manifestation of the site, was conceived as the sovereign in whose name the human ruler governed. In the 7th century BC, King Aššurbanipal still used the phrase in a praise hymn to the god: 'Aššur is king, Aššur is king and Aššurbanipal is his representative!' The regent of Aššur shared power with the collective citizen body in the city assembly and with an official chosen yearly called *līmum*, whose name was used to date the year (e.g. *'līmum* of Ennam-Aššur' for 1760 BC), in a practice attested elsewhere in the ancient world in communities with a strong tradition of collective government (Athens, e.g. 'archonship of Solon' for 594 BC; Rome, e.g. 'consulship of Caesar and Bibulus' for 59 BC). Especially well attested is the period of the 19th century BC when family-run merchant firms based in Aššur established a network of profitable trading colonies in Anatolia. Throughout that time the designation 'Assyrian' referred only to the city of Aššur and its inhabitants.

The birth of Assyria

From the 18th century BC onwards, Aššur came again under the direct control of larger regional states but retained a strong cultural identity. The age of the city-state embedded in larger political structures came to an end when Aššur's last sovereign power Mittani (Hanigalbat to the Assyrians) went into decline in the 14th century BC. The rulers of Aššur used the power vacuum to establish their city as the centre of a territorial state that incorporated most of what is today northern Iraq. For the first time, they adopted the title of king. Their realm became the dominant power of northern Mesopotamia as they deftly played the game of international diplomacy, carefully navigating relations with states like Babylonia and Egypt to further their own ends.

The triangle between Aššur, Nineveh, and Arbela constituted the heartland of a state that subsequently governed much of the Middle East. Whenever regions were integrated as provinces, their inhabitants were counted as 'Assyrians', justified ideologically by their contribution to the worship of the god Aššur. By the late 13th century BC, Assyria controlled most of Mittani's former holdings. The western borders of the kingdom reached the Euphrates and the realm asserted itself politically and on the battlefield over its competitors in the south and north-west, the Babylonian and Hittite kingdoms.

When these states weakened and, in the case of the Hittite kingdom, completely disintegrated during the time of the great migrations marking the end of the Late Bronze Age, the political and social organization of their former territories changed drastically. Assyria, too, incurred territorial losses but maintained control over its well-protected heartland without any significant threats to the Assyrian monarchy and the kingdom's structure. In political discourse, the Arameans, one of the populations attested by sources of the 11th century BC to have been on the move, were cast in the role of the destructive intruders, whose unlawfully snatched territories must be absorbed back into the kingdom of Assyria, their rightful owner.

The creation of an empire

Unlike the adjoining regions, Assyria had never lost its chariot troops and could afford to maintain this specialized branch of the armed forces financially and socially. This and the realm's extent, greatly exceeding that of the neighbouring states, gave the kingdom an advantage in its subsequent wars of conquest. They began in the 10th century, when contemporary Assyrian sources prominently cite the duty to recreate the lost realm and to rescue those Assyrians who had been left behind the retreating borders. By the mid-9th century BC, Assyria's former maximum extent had been re-established. The state in the resultant form is today called the 'Assyrian Empire'. Its political organization was profoundly transformed in the king's favour by the creation of the mega-city Kalhu as the imperial centre and a sustained and extensive programme of relocating its populations to best serve state interests.

A three-decade long period of territorial expansion meant that by 700 BC, the lands from the Mediterranean shore to Hamadan (Ecbatana) in Iran, from Cappadocia to the Persian Gulf were under direct Assyrian control. Until the late 7th century BC, the empire was the unrivalled political, economic, and cultural power of the Middle East and the wider Eastern Mediterranean region.

The end of the empire

Then, however, Nabopolassar, king of the recently independent former client kingdom of Babylonia, and a Median army led by Cyaxares, began a decade-long war. In 614 BC the city of Aššur was captured and the temple of its god destroyed, followed in 612 BC by the loss of the then capital Nineveh and the life of the last rightful king Sin-šarru-iškun, who died defending his city and empire. Based in the city of Harran, the defence of the empire continued under the crown prince for a few more years. However, as he could no longer be crowned in the Aššur temple, the sacred custom that confirmed the king as the deity's representative and served as the ideological backbone of the imperial claim to power was painfully disrupted. As Aššur-uballit II, a name surely deliberately chosen to invoke the first Assyrian king of the 14th century BC, this last ruler was crowned in the temple of the moon god of Harran, one of the greatest Assyrian deities. But while this was good enough for Babylonian commentators, contemporary Assyrian sources suggest that he was still only considered the crown prince. The lack of Aššur's blessing must have severely damaged the authority of this last Assyrian ruler and not even the military support of allies from Egypt and the Iranian kingdom of Mannea could save the empire.

Most of the Assyrian heartland's population was resettled in Babylonia where Nabopolassar and his successor Nebuchadnezzar transformed their capital Babylon into an imperial centre to rival its Assyrian prototypes in Kalhu, Dur-Šarrukin, and Nineveh. No one took over the maintenance of these cities, whose enormous size and population could only be upheld with extensive and expensive regional irrigation systems supporting the fresh water supply. Without upkeep, the canals and aqueducts soon became dilapidated, never to be used again. At Nineveh, the bodies of those killed defending the city were never cleared away, as gruesome discoveries at Nineveh's Halzi Gate illustrate. At Kalhu, bodies of executed men were dumped in the well providing the citadel with drinking water, which illustrates a desire to destroy and spoil, rather than appropriate, the Assyrian heartland.

Assyrian history after the empire

Assyrian history was not over, though. On the one hand, it continued in exile. In the southern Babylonian city of Uruk, a group of Assyrian expatriates maintained in the 6th century BC a small shrine devoted to god Aššur, and much later, in the 2nd century BC, when the city was part of the Seleucid Empire, typical Assyrian traditions in cult and scholarship were still practised. And in Aššur, the temple of its god was re-established after 539 BC, albeit on a much more modest scale. According to the Cyrus Cylinder, having conquered Babylonia, Cyrus the Great, king of Persia, granted permission to do so:

> From Babylon I sent back to their places, to the sanctuaries across the river Tigris whose shrines had earlier become dilapidated, the gods who lived therein: to Aššur, Susa, Akkad, Ešnunna, Zamban, Meturan, Der, as far as the border of Gutium (i.e. Zagros mountain range). I made permanent sanctuaries for them. I collected together all of their people and returned them to their settlements.

In this small shrine, documents pertaining to the god and his sanctuary from the early second millennium BC until its destruction in 614 BC were assembled and demonstrate a keen awareness and appreciation of the city's glorious past. In the 1st century AD, when Aššur had found wealth and prominence as a trading centre in the kingdom of Hatra, the shrine was again rebuilt on monumental scale.

At that time, there was already a well-established Christian community at Hatra (Bardaisan, *Liber legum regionum* 46), and perhaps Christianity was also practised in Aššur. In any case, while the new temple and Aššur's cult fell victim to the Sassanian conquest of the kingdom of Hatra in about AD 240, the Eastern Churches flourished subsequently and local Christian traditions found new roles for prominent figures and sites of Assyrian history, quite separate from the information recorded in the Bible. Hence, the city of Aššur and King Sennacherib appear in the legend of the 4th century AD martyr, Saint Behnam, who converted to Christianity after local holy man Saint Matthew (in Aramaic, Mar Mattai) had miraculously healed his sister. Sennacherib was cast as Behnam's royal father who ordered the prince's execution. In turn, the king was struck by a disease and only cured when he agreed to be baptized by Saint Matthew in the city of Aššur. Grateful, Sennacherib then founded the monastery of Deir Mar Mattai near Mosul, one of the centres of the Maphrianate of the East (i.e. the Syriac Orthodox Churches east of the Euphrates). Today, Syriac Christian groups of the Eastern Church from the former Assyrian heartland (Nestorians and Jacobites) identify themselves as 'Assyrians'. The origins of this view remain a matter of debate but they pre-date the spectacular archaeological discoveries of the mid-19th century that put Assyria on the map for the rest of the world.

Chapter 2
Assyrian places

In this chapter we encounter the city where everything started and the city where the empire of the first millennium first came together: Aššur and Kalhu are two of Iraq's most significant archaeological sites. A glimpse at the trading colony at Kaneš in Central Turkey will enable us to investigate Assyrian history of the early second millennium BC further afield, while Dur-Katlimmu, an important provincial centre in Syria, will serve to emphasize the impact of Assyria's expansion from the 13th century BC onwards. The story of the exploration of those key sites will give insight into Assyria's rediscovery since the mid-19th century.

Aššur: the god and his sacred city

The city of Aššur (Figure 1) is situated at the southern edge of the core region of the Assyrian kingdom, a triangle formed by its three most important cities: Aššur, Nineveh in the north, and Arbela in the east. The Assyrian heartland covers an area of roughly 4,000 square kilometres and corresponds in size to, for example, the US state of Rhode Island (4,000 km²) or, in Britain, the county of Suffolk (3,800 km²). At the triangle's northern tip, underneath the urban sprawl of northern Iraq's largest city Mosul, lie the ruins of ancient Nineveh which have been excavated, on and off, since 1842. Nineveh oversees an important ford across the Tigris that is the natural terminus of the overland route leading along the

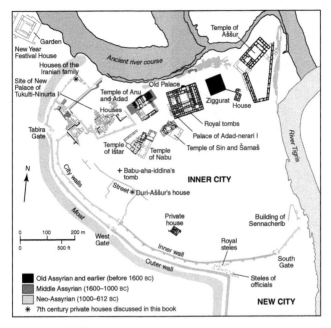

1. The city of Aššur.

southern foothills of the Taurus mountain range to the
Mediterranean coast and into Anatolia. At the triangle's eastern
tip, Arbela has kept its ancient name until today; as Erbil, it is
now the capital of the Kurdish Autonomous Region of Iraq. The
exploration of its archaeological heritage began only recently in
2006. Arbela is located on the western fringes of the Zagros
mountain range and controls various routes across the mountains
into Iran. Like Nineveh, the city of Aššur lies at an important
Tigris ford, but on the western riverbank. Situated in a
strategically excellent position on a rocky outcrop rising high over
a bend in the river, the site is a natural fortress. From there, one
controls the overland route leading west across the steppe into the
valleys of the Khabur and the Euphrates, and from there into
western Syria or across the Taurus mountains into Anatolia.

The Assyrian heartland occupied an important node of the overland trade network for the metals indispensable to the Middle Eastern economy. Tin, together with copper, was essential for the manufacture of the binary alloy bronze, the preferred material for tools and weapons from the fourth until well into the first millennium BC. From the Central Asian mines in what is today Afghanistan, Uzbekistan, and Tajikistan, tin was transported across Iran and into modern Iraq within easy reach of the Assyrian triangle. Silver was the preferred currency of the ancient Middle East and came primarily from Anatolian deposits, the fabled 'Silver Mountains'. The regions immediately to the north and east of the Assyrian heartland are occupied by the mountain ranges of Taurus and Zagros, which offer iron ore, timber, and stone as well as pasture for cattle and horses. Westwards lie the steppe lands of al-Jezira (the 'island' between Euphrates and Tigris); good grazing grounds for sheep. To the south lies Babylonia in the flood plain of Euphrates and Tigris whose promise of prosperity is closely linked to its ability to maintain large-scale and labour-intensive artificial irrigation through a network of canals, and therefore to the political organization of the region.

With the notable exception of Aššur, the Assyrian heartland lies on the eastern bank of the Tigris. Part of the Mediterranean climate zone, its agriculture is rain-fed and therefore fundamentally different from that of Babylonia, which is entirely dependent on artificial irrigation. The region is a natural breadbasket, nourished by very good soils in a flat physical environment favourable for large-scale cultivation. The main crops were barley and wheat, which were harvested in autumn. Aššur is situated on a geo-ecological border where the favourable Mediterranean climate gives way to the arid steppe zone. As the only central Assyrian city situated on the western bank of the Tigris, Aššur was a key contact point with the pastoralists who made use of this dry region with their sheep flocks, and its geographical position favoured its function as a trading centre. The city emerges as an important emporium most clearly in the texts dating to the early second

millennium BC. The relatively limited material available from
Aššur is complemented by the extremely rich textual sources from
one of its trading colonies in Anatolia at the city of Kaneš.

The god Aššur

Assyria's self-designation from the 14th century BC onwards is the
'land of Aššur' (*māt Aššur*). We call this state Assyria, using the
Greek term. This obscures some of the nuances of its original
name that refers as much to the city of Aššur, the state's original
centre and the place of origin of its ruling dynasty, as to the deity
of the same name whose ancient temple dominated that city. The
god Aššur and the city of Aššur are inseparable, as the deity is the
personification of the rocky crag called Qal'at Sherqat in Arabic
that towers high above a bend of the river Tigris. Shaped like the
prow of a ship, the roughly triangular crag rises 40 metres above
the valley, providing shelter and opportunities for the people who
settled there since at least the mid-third millennium BC. As the
city developed, the natural defences provided in the north and
east by the rock cliffs and the Tigris below were completed with
a crescent-shaped fortification wall, resulting in an enclosed area
of *c.*65 hectares.

Popular Assyrian names, such as Aššur-duri, 'The god Aššur is my
fortress'; Dur-makî-Aššur, 'A fortress for the weak is the god Aššur';
Aššur-nemedi, 'The god Aššur is my base'; or Aššur-šaddî-ili, 'The
god Aššur is a divine mountain', illustrate that the deity could be
perceived as a very concrete space. A stone relief from the early
second millennium BC (Figure 2) depicts Aššur accordingly: using
the typical scale design reserved for mountains in Assyrian art, it
shows the god as a rocky peak from which the torso of a bearded
man emerges, accompanied by two deified fountains and sprouting
plants that nourish two goats, the emblematic animals of the deity.

Aššur's shrine at the top of the crag was the heart of the city and later
the land of Aššur. It was known under several names: as

2. Stone relief depicting the god Aššur and two deified springs. From Aššur.

Eamkurkurra 'The House of the Wild Bull of the Lands' in the early second millennium and as Ehursagkurkurra 'House of the Mountain of the Lands' in the later second millennium, and as Ešarra 'House of the Universe' in the first millennium BC. These names are all in the Sumerian language that was spoken in the south of Iraq in the

12

third millennium, when the city of Aššur was first founded, and later continued to be used in ritual and scholarship.

As the site of the one and only temple of the god, the city of Aššur was the nucleus of his realm and for millennia, and the inhabitants cared for the sanctuary until its last manifestation was destroyed in *c.* AD 240. In the 12th century BC, a ruler called Ušpia, thought to have lived a millennium earlier, was credited with the construction of the earliest version of the huge temple complex that at that time occupied the top of the crag. The Assyrian ruler was considered Aššur's human agent, invested by the deity's grace with the power to rule and at the same time also his head priest, lending him religious as well as political authority. Ušpia and his successors had the privilege and duty to care for the god's temple and numerous inscriptions found in the sanctuary celebrate building work undertaken at the sanctuary.

Excavating Aššur

The sanctuary of Aššur was explored during the German excavations from 1903 to 1914 led by Walter Andrae who lived and worked there for over a decade, investigating Aššur and nearby sites with the help of a few assistants, usually, like Andrae himself, architects by training, and hundreds of local workmen. In Iraq, specialized archaeological excavators are called Sherqatis because the profession originated with Andrae's workers at Qal'at Sherqat. Most of the objects unearthed during these excavations are now in the Vorderasiatisches Museum in Berlin and in the Oriental Museum in Istanbul, as the finds were divided between the German Oriental Society that funded the work and the Ottoman authorities who controlled Iraq at that time. In addition to some German excavations, Iraqi teams have continued sporadically with the exploration of Aššur since 1978, but it is Andrae's many years of uninterrupted work at the site that forms the basis of our detailed knowledge of the city. Andrae excavated the northern part of the site where the Aššur temple complex, including its massive stepped tower, is surrounded by other sanctuaries and the royal palaces. Trained as an architect, his main objective was to recover the ground plans of these monumental structures and to reconstruct their building history. But he also wanted to understand the city as a whole and therefore methodically excavated trenches, 10 metres wide, across the entire site, one every 100 metres. In this way, he uncovered parts of many private houses from the last period of the Assyrian Empire. When Aššur was captured in 614 by the forces of Cyaxares, king of the Medes, many of these houses were set on fire—in contrast to the monumental buildings which were thoroughly looted before their destruction, the excavation of the private quarters has yielded a great many finds, including clay tablets that were baked in the fires and thus ideally conserved. These texts, in the main legal documents but also letters and in some cases substantial libraries of scholarly and literary compositions, provide exceptional insight into the lives of Aššur's inhabitants in the 7th century BC. We will encounter some of them in chapters 3 and 5.

The houses had underground tombs where the dead of the family were buried, usually constructed underneath the innermost room where the family's archive was kept. The crypts were preserved even when the houses were rebuilt or razed. Andrae uncovered several dating back to the second millennium BC, including in 1908 the very rich burials of men and women of the family of Babu-aha-iddina ('Tomb 45'), part of whose archive was discovered near the entry shaft leading to the underground vault. The letters and administrative texts document the private business activities of this high-ranking state official who served under several kings in the 13th century BC and draw attention to the household's broad range of specialized manufacturing, which concentrated on creating expensive finished products such as perfumes, chariots, composite bows, and luxury leather and textile goods, using rare materials procured over large distances. The beautiful objects with which two bodies, thought to be Babu-aha-iddina and his wife, were placed on the remains of the earlier family burials include elaborate jewellery of gold and precious stones, intricately carved ivory combs, pins, and containers, and sumptuously decorated stone vessels—giving a vivid impression of the luxurious lifestyle that the Assyrian elite enjoyed at a time when the kingdom had become the leading political power of the Middle East.

The one temple of the god Aššur

One of the main objectives of Walter Andrae's excavations was the exploration of the Aššur temple. But his investigation barely reached the earlier parts of the sanctuary because they are covered by massive later constructions, all executed in mud-brick, the traditional Middle Eastern building material. The oldest connected structures that Andrae was able to uncover date to the beginning of the second millennium BC, at a time when income from the booming trade colonies in Anatolia swelled the coffers of the city. The earliest building inscriptions recovered from the temple date to the period of the foundation of these colonies and were written in the name of Erišum I. They describe how this ruler dedicated a new throne for the god Aššur and how private houses were cleared away in order to increase the area reserved for the sanctuary. About the Aššur shrine, Erišum writes:

> The name of that temple is 'Wild Bull', the name of the door is 'Protective Goddess', the name of the lock is 'Be Strong!' and the name of the threshold is 'Be Alert!'

The sanctuary and its constituent parts were considered animate, even sentient. They and all objects used in the temple were created and maintained by expert craftsmen: builders, carpenters, smiths, goldsmiths, scribes, and others. The temple craftsmen were also responsible for the fashioning and awakening (with a ritual called the 'Opening of the Mouth') of the statues of Aššur and the other gods revered at the city. Some had their own temples, like Ištar, the goddess of sex and battle, of whose repeatedly rebuilt shrine Andrae's excavations managed to expose the inner sanctuary of the early third millennium, with the stone statues of the goddess's worshippers lining its walls. The storm god Adad and the sky god Anu shared a temple as did the moon god Sin and the sun god Šamaš, but most deities were worshipped in Aššur's vast sacred complex.

Over time, as the Assyrian realm grew, more and more gods came to 'live' in the Aššur temple, in part the result of the practice of seizing the divine statues of defeated enemies and relocating them in Aššur's shrine. So long was the list of the temple's occupants by the first millennium BC that a learned text called today the Divine Directory of Aššur was composed to chart the complex topography of the sanctuary. The statues of gods were seen as manifestations of the deities, and by staying as Aššur's guests, or hostages, in his home, these gods accepted, for all to see, Aššur's sovereignty. When in c.700 BC King Sennacherib, for example, captured statues of Attar-šamayin, Day, Nuhay, Rudaw, Abir-ilu, and Attar-qurumâ, 'the gods of the Arabs', from the oasis of Adummatu (Dumat al-Jandal in Saudi-Arabia) and placed them in the Aššur temple, this had immediate political implications for the Arab tribes. They found themselves deserted by their gods who moreover seemed to recognize Aššur as their host and overlord. The strategy of god-napping was designed to persuade enemies or reluctant allies to follow their deities' lead and to accept Assyrian dominion. It was often successful, as in this case.

It was the privilege and duty of the servants of Aššur to provide their god with regular sacrifices that were presented to him in the form of a daily feast. Sheep, cattle, and poultry and other ingredients for these meals, namely barley, wheat, emmer (hulled wheat), sesame, honey, and seasonal fruit including apples and figs, were periodically delivered from all regions of his dominion to the sanctuary. These ingredients were not especially rare and could easily have been procured by other means. That they had to be provided, in relatively small quantities but regularly, from all across the realm, sometimes over vast distances, may have made little logistic sense but was of paramount ideological importance: all subjects of Aššur had to participate jointly in the care for the god. In this way, the realm was defined as the community of Aššur's worshippers. Conversely, the refusal to provide for the god's meal was of course considered an act of treason.

Once the ingredients arrived at Aššur, the temple's butchers, bakers, brewers, and oil-pressers—all of them men—processed the materials and prepared the dishes that were then served to Aššur. Culinary specialists may perhaps not immediately match commonly held connotations of priesthood, but in a context where the ritual preparation and celebration of a daily feast in honour of the deity was at the core of temple worship, they were naturally among the priestly personnel. Like the craftsmen responsible for temple and cultic objects, all kitchen staff had to be ritually pure in order to interact so intimately with the deity. As a visible marker of their purity, all temple staff had to be clean-shaven. Whereas other Assyrian men typically sported shoulder-length hair and full beards (except for the eunuchs who served the empire in key roles from the 9th century BC onwards), the temple staff had to be bald and without facial hair. Only in the 7th century BC were these rules somewhat relaxed, and some of Aššur's kitchen staff 'stood with hair' for several years before they were shaven.

In 1911 Andrae found more than 650 clay tablets in one of the buildings of the temple complex for Aššur, archived in ten large ceramic containers, which held parts of the records of four successive temple administrators responsible for the organization of the god's meals in the 12th and early 11th century BC. When the building was structurally modified at a time when these records were no longer relevant, the heavy pots were simply left in place and buried within the new construction. As the documents record deliveries from all twenty-seven provinces constituting the kingdom, they allow the detailed reconstruction of the political organization of

Assyria, encompassing at that time the lands from the Euphrates to the Lower Zab. Even when the royal court and the centre of political power and government were moved away from Aššur in the imperial period—to Kalhu in 879 BC, then to Dur-Šarrukin in 706 BC, and finally to Nineveh around 700 BC—the feast of Aššur continued to be organized in the established way by involving all provinces (about seventy-five by the 670s BC). As administrative texts found at the royal palace in Nineveh demonstrate, organizing Aššur's menu remained a matter of state importance.

As gods were thought to consume their meals by smelling, the 'leftovers' of Aššur's feast, as the dishes were called once they had been removed from the offering table, could be further distributed. A strict protocol governed who received which parts of the leftovers, with cuts of meat being considered the most prestigious. The Assyrian ruler, regarded as the earthly representative of the god Aššur, naturally topped the list of recipients that embraced temple staff and dignitaries from across the realm, including the provincial governors. In order to reach these, the dishes had to be transported over considerable distances, just as had previously the ingredients from which they had been prepared. That the food was no longer fresh was not an issue, as to eat from the divine feast was a blessing rather than a culinary experience: 'Whoever eats the leftovers will live,' as one royal official puts it in the 7th century BC. Partaking in Aššur's meal in this manner was a huge privilege and bound the Assyrian officials together and to the god, no matter how far away from his temple they were based. Even when abandoned as the political centre after 879, the city of Aššur never lost its fundamental ideological importance.

The city of Aššur after Assyria

The temple quarter of Aššur was called Libbali 'Heart of the City', a designation first attested in texts of the 13th century BC, although very likely older. The name came to be used as a synonym for the entire city, presumably as this avoided confusion with god and country. According to the geographical compendia of Ptolemy of Alexandria (2nd century AD; as Labbana) and Stephen of Byzantium (6th century AD; as Libana) and possibly also the Tabula Peutingeriana (AD 1200 copy of an original Roman map; misspelt as Sabbin), the city was still known under this name much later in the Roman imperial period when it was part of the kingdom of Hatra. At that time, the cult of Aššur (now called Assor) continued to be practised according to the by now millennia old traditions and festival calendar, albeit with a contemporary veneer. The temple had been rebuilt in modern Parthian-style architecture and the inhabitants of the city now invoked the deity with their Arabic, rather than Assyrian, names. But the cult was of local importance only and it was the city lords, rather than the kings of nearby Hatra, who were the patrons of the sanctuary. They saw themselves firmly in the tradition of the Assyrian kings of old, as perhaps best illustrated by the inscribed steles erected in the gateway leading to the Assor temple. They share the typical rounded shape of the Assyrian royal steles (see Figure 8) and show city lords like R'uth-Assor ('Joy of Aššur') in the same gesture of prayer as the Assyrian kings on their monuments, albeit in a Parthian-style trouser suit rather than the traditional Assyrian shawl garment and with an inscription in alphabetic Aramaic instead of Assyrian cuneiform (Figure 3).

The invasions of the kingdom of Hatra under the Sassanian kings Ardashir I and Shapur I from AD 240 onwards led to the violent destruction of the Assor temple and the entire city and the dispersal of its inhabitants. In later periods, the crag often served as a fortress, most recently in Ottoman times—small wonder, given its excellent strategic position. But the sanctuary and the cult of Aššur were never revived, although the desolate remnants of the ruined stepped tower of the Assyrian temple serve even now as a haunting reminder of the time when this great shrine was the religious hub of an empire stretching from the Mediterranean to Central Iran.

3. Stele of R'uth-Assor, Master (Maryo) of Labbana/Assor.

Kaneš: a 'harbour' in Central Turkey

Long before sacrifices for the god Aššur reached his city from regions beyond the Taurus Mountains, treaties were sworn in his name to protect the interests of his city and its inhabitants. According to these, Aššur is not the unrivalled master of the universe who stipulates his will. Instead, he stands on equal footing with the deities who were thought to guide and guard the other parties: the rulers of the Anatolian principalities in the early second millennium BC. As agreed in these treaties and protected by oath, the local leaders allowed the Assyrian traders free passage and, depending on the location, the right of residency in a trading colony in return for a cut of their profits.

One of the most important treaty partners was the ruler of Kaneš, today one of the best-explored archaeological sites in Central Turkey. It is situated about 20 kilometres from the modern city of Kayseri and dominates a fertile plain where several long-distance routes meet that connect western and northern Anatolia with Syria. The site's modern name Kültepe means 'ash mound'. This refers to the fact that during its long existence from *c.*3000 BC to the early Roman period, the ancient settlement was repeatedly destroyed by fire, which left behind huge ash layers. As always in this case, this proved beneficial for the survival of the clay tablets used as writing material by the city's inhabitants in the early second millennium BC, because they were baked and conserved in this way. In 1881 the first cuneiform texts from Kültepe came to the attention of scholars who called them 'Cappadocian tablets', after the classical name for the Central Anatolian plateau, as this was all that was known about their origin. Written in an early dialect of Assyrian and in a particular form of the cuneiform script that used fewer than 200 characters, the tablets' contents allowed them to be linked to the city of Aššur. The realization that merchants from northern Iraq had established colonies some 1,000 kilometres away from their city caused great interest in the tablets and in the puzzle of their origin.

But for over forty years, the local people who periodically dug the tablets up at Kültepe (Figure 4) and sold them to antiquities dealers managed to keep their source a secret, despite the fact that several archaeological missions investigated the site, always focusing their attention on the high mound. The locals had discovered the tablets when digging for ancient mud-brick, traditionally used throughout the Middle East as fertilizer and building material—to the dismay of archaeologists, as this practice is very destructive. Some 2,500 tablets were unearthed and bought up by various European and American museums and private collectors. Only in 1925, the mystery of the origin of the Cappadocian tablets was solved by the drunken indiscretion of a local coachman in the employ of Bedřich Hrozný, the Czech orientalist famous for his decipherment of Hittite, which he identified as an Indo-European language. Hrozný had recently started excavations at Kültepe and when his driver revealed that the tablets did not come from the

4. Satellite image of Kültepe, showing the extent of the excavations: the palaces and temples of Kaneš on the circular high mound and the merchant quarters in the lower town adjoining the mound in the north-east.

mound but from a site in the lower town, his team quickly found over a thousand tablets in what turned out to be the ruins of the Assyrian merchant quarters. Since 1948 the mound and the lower town have been investigated in yearly excavations under the auspices of Türk Tarih Kurumu, the Turkish Historical Society founded by Mustafa Kemal Atatürk in 1930 to promote the study of Turkey's past. The exploration of Kültepe is among the organization's flagship activities and profoundly shaped by the life's work of Ankara archaeologist couple Tahsin and Nimet Özgüç who excavated there from 1948 to 2005. The finds from the site are kept in the Museum of Anatolian Civilizations at Ankara, with highlights on display in the fine gallery devoted to Kültepe.

The Assyrian tablets allow the identification of Kültepe with the city of Kaneš. With an area of over 20 hectares and a height of *c.*20 metres, its circular high mound is one of the largest in central Anatolia. The walled enclosure of a lower town takes up a crescent-shaped area of more than 100 hectares surrounding the high mound from the north, east, and south. The settlement is therefore considerably larger than the city of Aššur. Judging from the limited area of just under 9 hectares where Assyrian clay tablets are being found, the merchants from Aššur inhabited a particular quarter of this extensive lower town that was in the main populated by local people. The texts identify the Assyrian quarter as 'The Harbour' (*kārum*) of Kaneš, using the usual Assyrian word for a trading post; in the Middle East these were typically established in a waterside setting, albeit not in the case of Kaneš. In contrast to the three-millennia long occupation of the mound, the lower town was used only in the first part of the second millennium BC for a period of about three centuries. It was rebuilt several times and the houses of the Assyrian traders date to the lower town's settlement level II and, after a massive fire had engulfed the lower town, level Ib. The tablets found in these buildings constitute the archives of the Assyrian trading firms based at Kaneš. Assyrian texts from this period have been found elsewhere at a few sites in central Anatolia but amount to merely *c.*150 tablets and fragments in total, a tiny number compared to the staggering figure of 23,500 clay tablets recovered so far from Kaneš. The vast majority of these texts date to a period of about fifty years in the 19th century BC. Only 4,500 tablets have been published, mostly the early finds, with preliminary editions of another 5,000 texts from the Turkish excavations awaiting publication. Much remains to be done.

Assyrian trade in Anatolia

The archives of the Assyrian merchants at Kaneš allow the reconstruction of their business and private activities in amazing detail. They document the traders' lives at Kaneš, and especially the organization of their business enterprises, but also give insight into contemporary Aššur, where only very limited evidence for this period has been uncovered due to the fact that massive later occupational levels cover the relevant archaeological layers. Most of what we know about Aššur's political and social circumstances derives from the Kaneš material. Fortunately for us, the Assyrians based abroad were keen to stay closely informed about news from home and corresponded extensively with family members and business associates in Aššur, usually simply called 'The City' (*ālum*). The majority of known documents from Kaneš are letters. They consist of an inner tablet with the text, around which a thin coat of clay was wrapped as an inscribed envelope that identified sender and addressee and was impressed with the sender's seal but otherwise protected the confidentiality of the letter. This format is generally used for Assyrian letters and also in evidence for the later cuneiform correspondences of the second and first millennium BC.

During the roughly two centuries of the Assyrian traders' residence there, Kaneš was the capital of a regional state whose ruler, designated as 'prince' (*ruba'um*) by the Assyrians, resided in a palace on the fortified high mound. The lower town was structured by open squares and paved streets, underneath which sewage drains led away the wastewater. Six to eight two-storey houses, built back to back, formed the building blocks that made up the lower town's residential quarters. By far the best explored is the quarter inhabited by the Assyrians whose houses were built in the local style. Private buildings had a residential part with living rooms and kitchen and a smaller, lockable part where valuables were kept, including the cuneiform documents of the Assyrians, which were filed according to content and stored on shelves or inside containers (pots, wooden chests, or bags). The dead were typically buried with their grave goods in coffins or cist graves (resembling a stone-built box) underneath the houses, and this is also attested for the buildings occupied by Assyrians, although the texts indicate that they typically hoped to die and be laid to rest in Aššur.

The Assyrian traders specialized in the import of tin, procured in Aššur from distant supplies, and luxury textiles produced in that city and elsewhere by domestic manufacture. They transported these goods overland with caravans of donkeys, each carrying *c*.65 kilograms (=130 minas) of tin. The small but very heavy ingots were wrapped up in bales of fabric that were carefully balanced across the donkeys' backs and sides in order to spare them from discomfort and their owners from the expense of replacing ruined animals. Four-wheeled, ox-drawn carts with loading capacities of between 300 and 1,500 kilograms were used whenever good enough roads were available. Once at Kaneš, the merchants deposited their merchandise in the spacious storerooms of the palace up on the citadel, which, as the texts show, were used as central storage facilities. The strong-rooms in the traders' private houses will have mainly served to keep the silver and gold safe, into which the Assyrian traders converted their returns for the transport back to Aššur. But much of their economy functioned without cash purely on the basis of credit, anticipating key strategies employed in much more recent times by merchant banks.

The prince of Kaneš collaborated closely with the merchants, as he took a cut of all their business in return for residency rights and protection within his territory, both for the caravans and the Assyrians living there. They were not regarded as his subjects, as the merchant quarter was politically and legally considered an extraterritorial part of the city-state of Aššur. Even during local hostilities the caravans were to pass unharmed—the Assyrians, who had little military power (and certainly none in Anatolia), were keen to protect their neutrality. In turn, as stipulated by treaty, the prince was entitled to taxes of *c.*3 per cent on the imported tin (that is, 4 minas per donkey load) and of 5 per cent on the textiles, with the option of buying another 10 per cent of the fabrics at market price. The prince's treaty partner was 'the city of Aššur, the citizens of Aššur and the "harbour"', which was not just the physical location of the Assyrian trading quarter at Kaneš but also the name for the collective body of traders operating there.

The agreements between the prince of Kaneš and the Assyrian merchant collective can be reconstructed from references in various texts but are also laid down in detail in an original treaty tablet that was found in 2000 in one of the houses of the second occupational phase of the Assyrian merchant quarter (level Ib). The trader collective also conducted treaties with the rulers of the kingdoms that the caravans traversed on their way to Kaneš, such as Apum (region of modern Qamishli in north-eastern Syria) and Hahhum (region of the modern Turkish city of Samsat), where another Assyrian 'harbour' was located, this time indeed waterside near an important ford across the Euphrates. Recorded in another original treaty tablet found together with the one concerning Kaneš, the stipulations assuring free passage and protection intriguingly include a guarantee not to sabotage the ferry and sink the merchandise—an indication that such acts of river piracy might have otherwise come to pass. Instead of an outright entitlement to levy taxes, the dignitaries of Hahhum were given the right to buy certain quantities of the Assyrian caravans' tin and fabric at discounted prices.

Its favourable position in the overland route network made Kaneš a very good choice for the Assyrians to use as the central base of their commercial activities, with a network of smaller outlets administrated from there. It took the caravans five to six weeks to cover the distance of *c*.1,200 kilometres from Aššur to Kaneš. But the traders operated on a much larger geographical scope and maintained similar bases elsewhere at the capitals of over a dozen Anatolian realms. The most important are the 'harbours' at the cities of Durhumit, perhaps situated close to sizable copper deposits and the Black Sea in the plain of Merzifon (250 kilometres north of Kaneš), and Purušhaddum, now thought to correspond to Üçhöyük near Bolvadin (385 kilometres west of Kaneš). Transport costs and taxes, rather than time and distance, determined where business was going to be profitable. If the price was right the Assyrian merchants were willing to travel very far. Aššur's involvement in Anatolia ceased when the emergence of large territorial states robbed the trader collective of the legal and political basis making long-distance trade lucrative.

Kalhu: a capital fit for an empire

In 879 BC the city of Aššur was stripped of its traditional role as the seat of political power and state administration when King Aššurnasirpal II moved the court to a new location. His choice fell on Kalhu (Figure 5), an ancient city that was transformed into the unrivalled imperial centre during his reign and that of his son and successor Shalmaneser III.

Whereas Assyria's extent in the 9th century mirrored its boundaries in the 12th century BC, before the migrations at the end of the Bronze Age, its role in the wider region was now markedly different. It was an imperial power, no longer surrounded by states of comparable size and manpower but by much smaller principalities. Once Assyria had reclaimed the territories it had lost in the west and north, the state exceeded its

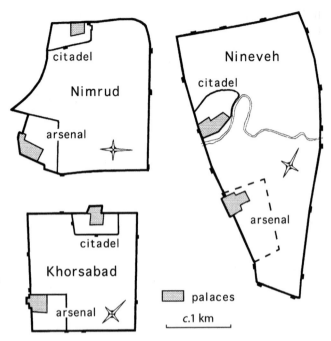

5. **The Assyrian capital cities Kalhu (Nimrud), Dur-Šarrukin (Khorsabad), and Nineveh.**

neighbours in extent and manpower many times over. The success of the reconquest allowed the Assyrian king to assume a new role of hegemon over his neighbours. Kalhu was conceived and created as the capital city for the new imperial power, its architecture designed to overwhelm and impress.

Kalhu is situated in a uniquely central position in the Assyrian heartland. It is very advantageously positioned inside the triangle formed by the three most important cities of Central Assyria and well connected to all of them: Aššur in the south, Nineveh in the north, and Arbela in the east. The city lies on the eastern bank of the Tigris, controlling a ford just north of its confluence with the Upper Zab. It has therefore direct access to the two principal waterways of the region and moreover a crossing over the Tigris, linking it to the west. On that river, Kalhu is located between Nineveh and Aššur and, thanks to a canal linking the city with the Upper Zab, there is also a direct river connection with Arbela. The distance from Kalhu to Aššur is *c.*70 kilometres, to Arbela *c.*60 kilometres, and to Nineveh *c.*35 kilometres as the crow flies. Travelling to and from either of these cities, therefore, takes a day, two at most, depending on the direction and the mode of travel, but in any case about half the time it takes to cover the distance between any of the three cities themselves. Moreover, Kalhu held an important position in the long-distance traffic network, both over land and on the rivers. It was a stop on the north–south route along the Tigris and controlled a key route leading in eastern direction via Arbela towards the Zagros Mountains and, along their western fringes, southwards into Babylonia.

Excavating Kalhu

Today, Kalhu's ruins are known as Nimrud, after a local tradition that connected the site to the Biblical figure of Nimrod, a grandson of Noah, who was the first human to claim kingship and credited with the foundation of Assyria. Nimrud is one of Iraq's most important archaeological sites.

Its investigation started in November 1845 with the British explorer Austen Henry Layard whose subsequent books on his travels and discoveries were extremely popular at the time of their publication and remain among the most readable travelogues documenting the Middle East. Inspired and guided by the work of pioneering Frenchman Paul Émile Botta at what turned out to be Sargon II's capital city of Dur-Šarrukin, Layard's very first scrapings on Nimrud's citadel mound immediately yielded inscribed stone reliefs from what was afterwards identified as the palace of King Aššurnasirpal II. By employing an approach borrowed from mining, Layard was able to explore much of that building through a system of tunnelling, despite the very modest funding available for his activities. This way of working had little in common with the careful archaeological excavation methods that Andrae first used in Aššur some sixty years later, but yielded fast and spectacular results, especially in the form of intricately carved wall reliefs and other stone sculptures. Layard at first mistakenly thought that he had found Nineveh at Nimrud, but he later excavated at the actual city of Nineveh, digging on the Kuyunjik mound. He continued his digs until 1851, mainly with the goal to find as many antiquities as possible that could be transported back to Britain.

For a few decades, Assyria captured the imagination of 19th century audiences. A stream of newspaper articles kept the public abreast of the discoveries of Layard, his associate Hormuzd Rassam, and other pioneers taking up work on Assyrian sites. The first public showing of Assyrian objects was held in 1847 at the Louvre in Paris, followed in 1852 by the exhibition of Layard's finds at the British Museum, both pulling enormous crowds. Subsequently, stone sculptures from Nimrud were put on permanent display in the Assyrian Gallery of the British Museum and elsewhere in the world, as surplus materials were passed on to other European and American museums and collections. When the first Assyrian artefacts arrived in Europe, the craze of public interest led to the mass manufacture of various Assyrian-inspired luxury products such as jewellery, silver cutlery, and fireplace ornaments.

The general curiosity in all things Assyrian and the quick publication of the Assyrian inscriptions found at Nimrud and elsewhere made attempting to decipher the cuneiform script a favourite challenge for the linguistically minded, greatly aided by the realization that Assyrian was a Semitic language, like Hebrew and Arabic. By 1857, a competition organized by the Royal Asiatic Society in London served to demonstrate publicly the decipherment of Assyrian. Since these heady days of Assyromania, excavations at Nimrud have continued, on and off, mainly conducted by British and Iraqi archaeologists, and while they tended to concentrate on the citadel mound, there has also been work conducted on Tell Azar, the second citadel mound, and in the lower city.

Nimrud's most famous excavator since Layard was arguably not a professional archaeologist but crime novelist Agatha Christie, whose husband Max Mallowan directed the British excavations between 1949 and 1957. She photographed and registered finds and notably repurposed her expensive skin lotion to clean and strengthen the fragile ivory carvings that once decorated elaborate palace furniture and luxury objects. By writing murder mysteries such as 'They Came to Baghdad' on site, she continued Layard's tradition of authoring best-sellers inspired by work at Nimrud. The excavations during the 19th century only resulted in the discovery of a single cuneiform clay tablet, presumably because the unfired clay tablets were not recognized. During Mallowan's time at Nimrud and afterwards, Kalhu yielded a number of important textual finds. Particular highpoints are the so-called Nimrud Letters, some 300 letters from the Assyrian state correspondence of kings Tiglath-pileser III and Sargon II, unearthed in 1952, and multiple copies of the covenant imposed in 672 BC by King Esarhaddon on his subjects, found in 1955.

The most spectacular discoveries at Nimrud are the result of routine conservation measures undertaken by the Iraqi Antiquities Service which led in 1988 and 1989 to the unexpected detection of three undisturbed royal tombs underneath Aššurnasirpal's palace. These housed the burials of several Assyrian queens of the 9th and 8th centuries BC whose sumptuous grave goods include over fifty kilograms of intricately crafted gold jewellery and luxury vessels made of gold and rock crystal, many with inscriptions. When excavated, bodies and garments were in relatively good condition, but although anthropological and fibre analyses were quickly

31

initiated, the start of the Gulf War in 1990 and subsequent trade sanctions have prevented the burials from being studied in the scientific detail that this extraordinary discovery merits. So far, the precious finds have only ever been on public display for very short periods of time. Most of the time they have been locked away in a bank vault, but in this way, they have survived Iraq's tumultuous recent history relatively unscathed. Whenever the time comes for the Iraq Museum in Baghdad to put these objects on permanent display, they will hopefully attract the public attention they so richly deserve.

Most of the archaeological exploration of Nimrud so far has concentrated on the first millennium BC. Only occasionally, earlier materials have been exposed. While the foundation of the settlement is thought to go back to the sixth millennium BC, small-scale excavations on the citadel mound have succeeded in unearthing pottery and flint finds going back to the beginning of the third millennium BC. But it is in the early second millennium BC, during the time of Samsi-Addu, that the city emerges clearly as a site of trans-regional significance. Known at the time as Kawalhum, it appears in texts from the palace archives of Mari in Syria, where Samsi-Addu had appointed his younger son as regent, as an important port on the Tigris, and a richly equipped stone tomb with a bronze battle-axe, found in 1854 on the citadel mound, dates to that same period. Once the kingdom of Assyria was established in the 14th century BC, the city was the capital of a province, a status that it held until the end of the 7th century BC when the state ceased to exist.

The king's city and the king's people

Kalhu's position within Assyria was most prominent during the time from 879 to 706 BC, when it was the political centre of the empire. The city was elevated to its new role not only at the expense of Aššur, which it replaced as the main residence of the king, but also at the expense of Nineveh and Arbela. Due to

Aššur's peripheral location within the Assyrian state, these cities were economic and political centres in their own right, of almost the same importance as Aššur and, at least in Nineveh's case, with their own royal palace. Just as the cult of Aššur regularly demanded the king's attention and presence, the special significance of the cults of Ištar of Nineveh and Ištar of Arbela for the state required the king to spend considerable amounts of time in these cities in order to take his place in their festivals. By elevating Kalhu to the new imperial centre, the influence of all three cities, and their inhabitants, within the state was substantially weakened.

One can easily argue that the creation of the new centre was part of a larger strategy designed to strengthen the position of the king at the expense of the old urban elites. While they had previously played an important role in the political life of the Assyrian state, the highest administrative and military offices were from now on reserved for a new cadre of civil servants, the eunuchs (*ša rēši*, literally 'He of the head', i.e. 'personal attendant' of the king, contrasted with uncastrated officials called *ša ziqni*, 'He of the beard'). It is unclear today what qualities or qualifications were looked for in a boy or who made the fundamental decision to turn him into a eunuch. Nor is anything known about the eunuchs' original family backgrounds—but there is no reason to think that being made a eunuch was considered a terrible fate and one cannot necessarily assume that future eunuchs were forced into this life. It is quite possible that the eunuchs were in fact members of the same old families who previously held political offices, perhaps younger sons who could not expect to inherit much. Being a royal eunuch guaranteed high social status and a place in the king's household for life. But by sacrificing their ability to father children, the eunuchs gave up family life for good. They did not marry and were without any distraction at the state's and the king's disposal—the perfect employees. In return, the royal family shouldered the obligations normally expected from one's family, including the funeral and the subsequent offerings necessary to guarantee well-being in the afterlife. Yet despite being so very close to royal power, a eunuch could never hope to become king. Assyrian kingship required a man to be perfect in all respects, and a eunuch, with his mutilated body, was therefore categorically excluded.

The residents of the new imperial centre were handpicked by one of the royal eunuchs, the Palace Overseer Nergal-apil-kumu'a, whom Aššurnasirpal appointed by edict to oversee the move to Kalhu. The city's development changed settlement patterns not only in the Assyrian heartland but all over the empire, as suitable settlers were chosen from all provinces. We can safely assume that only those who had showed enthusiasm for the king and his plans for the Assyrian state were picked, thus creating in 879 BC not just a new political centre, but one that was populated by loyal supporters of king and empire. By creating new patterns of authority and allegiance, both socially and geographically, Aššurnasirpal was successful in changing the power structures that had previously defined Central Assyria. The move to Kalhu reinforced and secured the pre-eminence of the king and the state administration and provided the emerging Neo-Assyrian Empire with one unrivalled centre and a guaranteed power base of loyal supporters.

Architecturally, the ancient city of Kalhu was completely transformed. In order to provide the water needed for the maintenance of the new mega-city, a regional canal system was constructed. No expense was spared as the gigantic building project was calculated to show off Assyria's wealth to the world. The old settlement mound, having grown to a substantial height in the course of its long occupation, was turned into a fortified citadel that housed the royal palace and temples. But despite its size, it occupied only a small part in the south-western corner of the much larger city. With an area of about 360 hectares, Aššurnasirpal's Kalhu covered an area the multiple of the surface of Aššur and was surrounded by a 7.5 kilometre-long fortification wall. A second fortified citadel mound in the south-eastern corner of the city housed the arsenal where military equipment was stored and the army mustered. This basic plan was used also for the subsequent Assyrian capitals. The temples established at Kalhu were dedicated to the most important deities of Assyria, such as Ištar (but in the guise of the Lady of Kadmuri, distinct from her manifestations in Nineveh and Arbela), Ninurta, and Nabu, but there was no shrine for Aššur whose only sanctuary remained in the city of Aššur. Kalhu's purpose was to celebrate the king, not Aššur, as the nucleus of the empire.

At the time of Aššurnasirpal, Kalhu's most impressive building was certainly his new royal palace, called today the Northwest Palace due to its position on the citadel. With a length of 200 metres and a width of 130 metres, this gigantic building dominated its surroundings and, in an inversion of the topography of Aššur, dwarfed the neighbouring temples. Colossal human-headed winged bulls, perhaps the most iconic expression of Assyrian imperial architecture (Figure 6), guarded the monumental gates and provided Layard with a formidable logistical challenge when he shipped some of them back to London. Cedar trunks imported from Lebanon, with a length of up to 30 metres they were the longest roof beams available anywhere, allowed the construction of halls of unprecedented dimensions. The palace was organized around three courtyards with state apartments, an administrative wing, and the private quarters of the royal family, where the underground tombs of the queens were uncovered. This ground plan became the template for representative buildings all over the Assyrian Empire, such as the mansion of Šulmu-šarri at Dur-Katlimmu (see Chapter 3). Huge alabaster slabs with engraved figures and inscriptions celebrated the king's achievements and lined the walls of the palace's state apartments (see Figure 12). In particular, the throne room where Aššurnasirpal received dignitaries from all over the empire and beyond was decorated with scenes of heroic conquest and its results, the spoils, tribute, and gifts from the subdued adversaries. According to the inscription of a stele that was erected

6. Colossal winged human-headed bull from King Aššurnasirpal II's Northwest Palace at Kalhu, excavated by A. H. Layard.

inside the palace, 69,574 persons participated in the inaugural celebrations for the new city, the inhabitants of Kalhu joined by people from all over the empire and 5,000 foreign dignitaries from the adjacent states. Aššurnasirpal wined and dined his guests for ten days in a feast whose menu is preserved on the stele: 17,000 sheep and cattle and twice as many ducks, geese, and pigeons were slaughtered, meaning that every participant could expect to eat half a bird and a very sizeable portion of mutton and beef. These main courses were supplemented by venison, fish, and (less to our taste) rodents, enormous quantities of vegetables, fruit, and spices, and a broad range of dairy products, while 10,000 tubs of beer and 10,000 skins of wine provided relief for the thirsty.

Kalhu served as the main residence of all Assyrian kings up to Sargon II, who moved the court to his new imperial capital of Dur-Šarrukin, 'The Fortress of Sargon', in 706 BC. Several of Aššurnasirpal's successors established their own palaces in addition to the Northwest Palace that continued to be used as the provincial governor's residence. Iraqi archaeologists only recently excavated the palace of Adad-nerari III in 1993. The palace of Tiglath-pileser III is today known prosaically as the Central Palace, but this does not do its ancient name justice: 'Palaces of joy which bear abundance and bless the king who made their structure everlasting', The ceremonial name given to the palace gateway makes it clear how Kalhu was seen not just as the centre of Assyria but of the entire world:

> Gates of justice which pass fair judgement on the rulers of the four
> corners of the world, which offer the tribute from the mountains
> and the sea, which admit the produce of mankind before the king,
> their lord.

The stone parts of both these palaces were ransacked in the 7th century to provide building materials for a new palace of Esarhaddon who spent much time in Kalhu. His building remained unfinished, but its unusual columned halls highlight Egyptian cultural influence after the conquest in 671 BC.

Dur-Katlimmu: life in the western provinces

To the Assyrians, Tell Sheikh Hamad, located on the eastern bank of the Khabur River in north-eastern Syria, was the city of Dur-Katlimmu, a provincial centre of importance in the kingdom of Assyria since the 13th century BC. When the wealthy dignitary Šulmu-šarri (see Chapter 3) resided there in the 7th century the city was also known under the Aramaic name Magdala ('Tower'). This reflects the fact that Aramaic, rather than Assyrian, was the language most widely spoken in the Assyrian Empire of the first millennium BC. This West Semitic language is closely related to Hebrew and Phoenician, and any speaker of Assyrian, also a Semitic language, would have been able to understand Aramaic fairly well—without necessarily mastering its grammatical nuances—and vice versa. Outside the Assyrian heartland, Aramaic was very probably also the most frequently used written language. But in contrast to the Assyrian-language texts that were recorded in cuneiform on clay tablets, Aramaic was written in alphabetic script on paper-like materials such as leather or papyrus: these only survive in very dry contexts, such as the caves in the Judaean desert where the vast majority of early Aramaic documents have been found (but from much later dates), and disintegrate otherwise.

From at least the 9th century BC, the Assyrian state employed both Assyrian and Aramaic for government purposes as a direct consequence of the integration of the western states where this language was widely spoken. The use of Aramaic is documented in the Assyrian heartland from the reign of Shalmaneser III onwards: characters of the Aramaic alphabet are painted on the glazed bricks used for his buildings in the capital city of Kalhu, probably as fitters' marks. In addition, palace reliefs and door decorations routinely depict pairs of scribes, one writing with a pen on a scroll and the other impressing signs with a stylus into the surface of a clay tablet or a multi-leaved wax-covered wooden tablet. These devices, too, did not usually survive the ravages of time. Some luxury versions made from ivory have been recovered from Aššur and Kalhu, but without the wax layer and therefore the text. Such wax tablets closely correspond to the famous Vindolanda Tablets from Hadrian's Wall, Britain's oldest surviving handwritten documents from the 1st and 2nd centuries AD; cuneiform scribes routinely used them ever since the third millennium BC.

The most important indications of the widespread use of Aramaic as a written language in the Assyrian Empire are, first, the alphabetic annotations incised or written in ink on clay tablets that record the transfer of property. These short notes summarize the content of the cuneiform contract, apparently for the benefit of those who could read Aramaic but were less familiar with Assyrian cuneiform (Figure 7). Secondly, there is a particular type of clay tablet that was inscribed with Aramaic text only. These debt notes use a very specific, triangular shape and were formed around a knotted string. It is unclear what was fixed to the other end of that string but most likely it was a version of the same debt note on an Aramaic-language scroll. The reason for this assumption is that the more frequently attested alternative format for debt notes consists of an inner tablet enclosed in a sealed clay envelope, both inscribed with identical text. The Aramaic clay triangles, too, are sealed and may therefore fulfil the function of the envelope vis-à-vis the hypothetical scroll. Whatever they are, very many such tablets as well as contracts with Aramaic annotations have been found at Dur-Katlimmu and they are also known from other sites in the western Assyrian provinces. In the heartland, they are considerably less frequent, presumably reflecting the much wider knowledge of cuneiform. Although the scribes writing private legal documents in Dur-Katlimmu produced very handsomely shaped and elegantly written tablets, they were certainly not native Assyrian speakers: their frequent

7. Property sale contract from Dur-Katlimmu in Assyrian cuneiform, with two lines of summary in alphabetic Aramaic incised above and below the two stamp seal impressions.

and very characteristic grammatical mistakes indicate that they were used to expressing themselves in a West Semitic language, most likely Aramaic.

Integrating the west into the kingdom of Assyria

A German team led by Hartmut Kühne has been exploring the site of Tell Sheikh Hamad in annual excavation campaigns since 1978, after the archaeological team mapping the Khabur valley's many sites in 1977 learned that local people had found a group of clay tablets. It turned out that when constructing a water reservoir on the settlement mound they had unwittingly exposed rooms of a building complex from where the city and its region were managed in the last part of the second millennium BC. In total, some 400 tablets have been recovered of an administrative archive of the 13th and early 12th century BC that deals with the running of the agricultural estates supporting the provincial government. The tablets were baked in the fire that had destroyed the building. Some texts were rendered illegible, as they came too closely into contact with the flames, and others were lost to the river when local children used the earliest finds, in an ingenious repurposing of the flat clay tablets that comfortably fit into one's hand, as skipping stones. The surviving texts also contain references to wooden writing boards, which of course have not been preserved.

Most of the extant texts are administrative documents that give much insight into the economic situation at Dur-Katlimmu, which lies in the 'risk zone' between the climate zones of the Mediterranean and the steppe. A local irrigation canal system supported the rain-fed agriculture and fostered production of good harvests of barley, wheat, and sesame, supplemented by vegetables and herbs. The work was performed by the 'farmers of the palace', managed by the provincial government. They maintained two herds of donkeys, totalling 150 head, as pack animals. Cattle, used in pairs to drag the seeder-ploughs and to supply milk and meat, grazed in the meadows by the river while shepherds took the flocks of sheep and goats into the steppe: their wool and hair (for felt) was the backbone of the local textile industry.

The Dur-Katlimmu documentation and the agricultural activities recorded therein closely correspond to what is known from the capital Aššur and other sites in the provinces, such as the nearby city of Harbe (Tell Chuera in Syria) and the smaller fortified settlements called *dunnu* at modern Giricano (Dunnu-ša-Uzibi; near the Turkish city of Diyarbakir) or Sabi Abyad (in the Syrian Balikh valley). This illustrates one aspect of how the expanding kingdom of Assyria brought its way of life to the newly integrated territories. The governor and his staff were dispatched from the centre to the provinces where they introduced administrative routines using the Assyrian language and script, as well as typical standard forms for all sorts of documents to organize the provincial government's economic base. A set amount of taxes had to be delivered from the provincial centres to the capital, including the ideologically important contributions of ingredients for the daily feast prepared for the god Aššur.

Within the kingdom of Assyria in the late second millennium BC, Dur-Katlimmu had a special position, as it was not merely the centre of a province but the pre-eminent city of the realm's western half. The second-highest dignitary of the kingdom resided here, the Chief Chancellor (*sukallu rabiu*) of Assyria, whose courtesy title was 'King of Hanigalbat', after the Assyrian designation for its former overlord Mittani. The first to hold this title was Ibašši-ili, a younger son of King Adad-nerari I and brother of his successor Shalmaneser I. Both these kings waged war against Mittani and brought its territories under Assyrian control. At that time, rather than appropriating one of the old Mitanni centres, Dur-Katlimmu was established as the centre of government. This ancient settlement was linked to the city of Aššur through a direct route (later part of the 'King's Road' network; see Chapter 6) that was the shortest connection from the capital to the new holdings in the Khabur valley. This gave the incentive for the city's elevation under Shalmaneser I who founded a temple for the god Salmanu there, a deity closely associated with the Assyrian royal family and celebrated by this king's name, which in Assyrian is rendered Salmanu-ašared 'The god Salmanu is eminent'. Salmanu's name means 'The Kind One' and perhaps he was merely a deified aspect of the god Aššur, whose intimate connection to the city of Aššur made building other temples in his own name awkward. A stele dating to the early 8th century BC, of which the first piece was recovered from Tell Sheikh Hamad in 1879 by Austen Henry Layard's associate Hormuzd Rassam, records how King Adad-nerari III and the local governor Nergal-ereš renovated the temple, using cedar logs procured from Lebanon during a military campaign to the Mediterranean:

> The old temple, which Shalmaneser (I), my ancestor (literally 'my father'), had built, had become dilapidated and I, in a stroke of inspiration, built this temple from its foundations to its parapets. I placed the cedar roof beams from Mount Lebanon on top.

Shalmaneser's brother Ibašši-ili passed on his new and powerful office of King of Hanigalbat to his descendants. When the main line of the Assyrian royal house became extinct in 1183 BC, after old King Tukulti-Ninurta I, who had occupied the throne for thirty-seven years, was assassinated by his sons who then became embroiled in violent succession conflicts, his great-great-grandson Ninurta-apil-Ekur became king of Assyria. So powerful was the new king's father Ili-pada that a Babylonian king addressed him and the actual king Aššur-nerari III, one of Tukulti-Ninurta's short-lived sons, insultingly as 'the kings of Assyria' in a letter that ridicules Assyrian impotence in the aftermath of the regicide:

> The god Aššur has made you, Aššur-nerari and Ili-pada, because of (your) irresponsibility, constant drunkenness and inability to make decisions, go crazy. There is no one among you who has any sense.

It was a Babylonian intervention that brought Ili-pada's son to the throne after his death, and all subsequent kings, until the end of the empire, were his descendants. When the 8th century ruler Adad-nerari III claimed Shalmaneser I as 'his father' in the stele from Dur-Katlimmu, a designation that Assyrian kings generally used for their predecessors, he was factually wrong as he was descended from Shalmaneser's brother Ibašši-ili.

In the period of the reconquest of the lost western regions in the 10th century BC, Dur-Katlimmu played a crucial strategic role as an Assyrian enclave. In the 9th century BC, a sizeable fortified lower town was added to Dur-Katlimmu, transforming it from a relatively small town into a 60 hectare large city with a fortification wall of almost 4 kilometres, traversed by a canal 9 metres wide—modest when compared to contemporary Kalhu with its 360 hectares, but by far the biggest settlement on the Khabur. Much of the archaeological work since 1978 has focused on this lower town, unearthing enormous mansions modelled on the imperial palace architecture. The best known of these, the so-called Red House (see Figure 9), dates to the 7th century BC and was the residence of military man and wealthy landowner Šulmu-šarri. The activities of Šulmu-šarri's heirs are documented even during and after the disintegration of the Assyrian Empire and illuminate the political situation in Dur-Katlimmu at the time. At first, just after 612 BC, the population was loyal to the Assyrian crown, but local power rested now in the hands of a 'city lord' rather than the members of the previous city administration. A decade later, the city accepted Babylonian sovereignty: four private legal documents that otherwise conform entirely to the Assyrian traditions are dated according to the regnal years of Nebuchadnezzar II. As the mention of his priest in two of these texts indicates, the temple of the god Salmanu was still active at the time.

Chapter 3
Assyrians at home

The following sketches illustrate the great variety of living conditions and human experiences in the Assyrian Empire. They have two things in common: they all date to the 7th century BC, the period when the source material is most numerous and diverse, and they all are situated in an urban context. This is not coincidental as the available sources all come from cities and tend to concern themselves with matters of urban life. We encounter a king, two scholars of a leading learned family, a wealthy landowner, and a wine merchant, as well as their families and households.

Master of the universe: King Esarhaddon

Of all kings of Assyria, Esarhaddon (Figure 8) is the one emerging most clearly as an individual from the available sources. Most Assyrian rulers are known primarily from their royal inscriptions. Written on the kings' behalf to commemorate their deeds, these texts were either inscribed on monuments (statues, steles, rock reliefs) or written into the fabric of temples, palaces, and city walls, visibly on walls and gates or ritually buried in foundation deposits. Their Assyrian designation means 'written names' and their purpose was to perpetuate their protagonists' existence beyond their physical existence. Their authors, royal scholars headed by the Chief Scribe, concentrated unashamedly on the king and his

8. Stele of Esarhaddon, king of Assyria, showing him on the front with the subjugated rulers of Tyre and Kush and on the sides his sons Aššurbanipal and Šamaš-šumu-ukin as crown princes of Assyria and Babylon, respectively.

deeds, focusing on what was expected of a ruler and pleasing to the gods: the building and maintenance of temples, palaces, and cities and the protection and expansion of the realm. Written during their protagonists' lifetime and with their authorization, such compositions present a sympathetic reading of their hero's life and times, excluding what did not serve to celebrate and impress.

For most of Assyrian history, royal inscriptions are our most prominent yet biased source. But this is not the case in the 8th and 7th centuries BC, when contemporary correspondence and administrative documents survive from the palaces at Kalhu and Nineveh, and from elsewhere; the 670s, when Esarhaddon ruled the empire, are an especially well-documented decade.

Esarhaddon was a younger son of Sennacherib, as indicated by his name, which means 'The god Aššur has given a brother (to the existing siblings)'. He became king of Assyria in 681, despite the fact that he had not been the original crown prince—the heir apparent to the throne, chosen by the king, confirmed by the gods, and appointed in public. When making Esarhaddon crown prince in 683, Sennacherib first had to dismiss his previous choice, heir apparent to the empire for well over a dozen years. This son, Urdu-Mullissi, remained at court, so it is unlikely he had fallen from grace completely, but Sennacherib's motives are unknown. He did not realize that his decision endangered his life, for Urdu-Mullissi now assembled supporters for a *coup d'état*. The plot was almost uncovered when an official, whom the conspirators had approached in vain, sought an audience with the king, but so widespread was the conspiracy that Urdu-Mullissi's cronies were able to intercept him. According to a letter later sent to Esarhaddon,

> They asked him: 'What is your appeal to the king about?' He answered: 'It is about Urdu-Mullissi.' They covered his face with his cloak (as was the custom when meeting the king) and made him stand before Urdu-Mullissi himself, saying: 'Look! Your appeal is being granted, say it with your own mouth!' He said: 'Your son Urdu-Mullissi will kill you.'

The conspirators promptly disposed of him and their plot came to fruition: in 681, Urdu-Mullissi and a brother stabbed their father to death. But the aftermath of the regicide saw friction between the conspirators and Urdu-Mullissi's coronation was delayed.

Nineveh was in chaos when Esarhaddon, absent at the time of the assassination, marched on the capital. He managed to drive out the murderers and ascended the throne two months after his father's death. These events caused a stir all over the ancient world, best illustrated by the Biblical accounts that also report the flight of the murderous princes to Urartu (2 Kings 19:37; Isaiah 37:38).

For well over a century, the empire had been locked in conflict with its northern rival and now, by sheltering pretenders with a good claim to the throne, Urartu gained substantial influence over Assyrian politics. Esarhaddon could not touch the leaders of the *coup d'état* and steered clear of Urartu throughout his reign. At home, he made every effort to ensure that his brothers had no powerful allies left, should they ever try to return from exile. Officials high and low who were suspected of sympathy for the enemy were replaced throughout the empire. Archival records from Nineveh and Kalhu show, for example, that the entire palace security staff was dismissed, and we may suspect that they were not sent into early retirement but executed. His bloody ascent to power shaped the new king profoundly and Esarhaddon was distrustful of all around him. Routine inquiries made every three months to the all-seeing sun god Šamaš, patron of justice and divination, were supposed to establish whether anyone wished him ill. But problematically, the prime suspects were those who were meant to support him in governing: state officials, members of the extended royal family, the military, palace staff, and the Assyrian allies who provided auxiliary troops for the empire's army. This is one of many such queries from late in Esarhaddon's reign, filed in copy together with the expert report on the autopsy of the liver of a sacrificed lamb that was thought to reveal the divine answer:

> Will any of the eunuchs or bearded officials, the king's courtiers,
> the members of the royal line, senior or junior, or any other relative
> of the king, or the military officers, recruitment officers, team

commanders, the royal guard, personal guards or the king's
chariaoteers, the keepers of the inner or outer gates, stable attendants,
domestic staff, cooks, confectioners, bakers, craftsmen, or ... (various
foreign) auxiliaries, or their brothers, sons or nephews, their friends
(literally, 'masters of salt and bread') or anyone who is acquainted
with them, be they eunuchs or bearded, any enemy at all, whether
by day or by night, or in the city or in the country, whether while
(Esarhaddon is) sitting on the royal throne or chariot or rickshaw,
walking, going out or coming in, eating or drinking, dressing or
undressing or washing himself, whether through deceit or guile or
any other means, make an uprising and rebellion against Esarhaddon,
king of Assyria? ... I ask you, great lord Šamaš, whether from today
6/XII to 5/III of the coming year they will rise and rebel against
Esarhaddon, king of Assyria, whether they will act in a hostile
manner against him or kill him.

The Assyrian allies listed in this query indicate that the empire's
power was greater than ever before. By force or by treaty, and often
both, the empire had acquired new partners that extended Assyrian
influence as far the Caspian Sea and Sudan and deep into the
Arabian Peninsula. Our text lists Elam and the Cimmerian horse
nomads in Iran, the polities along the Nile, including the kingdom
of Kush and Arabian tribes such as the Qedarites, who all became
tied to the empire. The completion of a peace treaty with Elam,
Assyria's long-standing rival in Iran, in 674 was a skilful political
manoeuvre that secured the empire's eastern borders. This provided
the first chance ever to invade Egypt, whose politically fragmented
landscape was then dominated by the Nubian Taharqa, king of
Kush in modern-day Sudan. Assyria's first attempted invasion in
673 resulted in a hasty retreat. But in 671, when the new Arab allies
were employed for an unexpected attack across the Sinai desert,
Egypt was conquered. Although reinforcing Assyrian supremacy
necessitated further campaigns (see Figure 11) in 667 BC and 664
BC, leading as far south as Thebes, the region was organized into a
unified Assyrian vassal state, first under the rule of Nekho of Sais
and then under his son Psammetikh.

All Assyrian rulers sought the sun god's advice, although due to the chances of preservation and recovery, the only queries surviving in the original are from the reigns of Esarhaddon and his successor Aššurbanipal. For the royal decision-making process, seeking divine council was crucial, as formulating the problem as a question and then interpreting the god's answer allowed a far more open discussion with officials and advisers than would otherwise have been possible in an absolute monarchy where no man was the almighty king's equal. The known queries cover a wide range of military and political matters such as appointments to key positions in state and court. But inquiries about possible betrayal survive only for Esarhaddon. His concern for security also shaped the way in which he had palaces in Nineveh and Kalhu redesigned: as impregnable fortresses.

A king in grief

Esarhaddon's inscriptions portrayed him in the traditional style as the solitary hero who triumphs all by himself. From his private letters, too, the king emerges as a lonely man, but in an altogether different way. The correspondence with the scholars in his entourage allows us detailed insight into his mental and physical state and shows that, despite his political and military successes, Esarhaddon was not a happy man. In 673 he experienced traumatic bereavement when he first lost his wife, the queen Ešarra-hammat and, shortly afterwards, their infant son during whose birth she may have died. As we read in a letter from his personal exorcist Adad-šumu-uṣur, one of the experts charged with caring for the king's well-being:

> As to what the king, my lord, wrote to me: 'I am feeling very sad; how did we act that I have become so depressed for this little one of mine?' – had it been curable, you would have given away half of your kingdom to have it cured! But what can we do? O king, my lord, it is something that cannot be done.

Esarhaddon was often ill, suffering from spells of fever and dizziness, violent fits of vomiting, diarrhoea, nosebleeds, and painful earaches. A permanent skin rash disfigured parts of his body and especially his face. Depression and fear of death cast a shadow on his life and for days he withdrew to his sleeping quarters, refusing food, drink, and human company. In one of his letters, Adad-šumu-uṣur tried to reason with his royal patient:

> Why is the table not brought to the king, my lord, today already for the second day running? Who would stay in the dark much longer than (the sun god) Šamaš, the king of the gods, stays in the dark, a whole day and night, and again two days? The king, the lord of the world, is the very image of Šamaš. He should keep in the dark for half a day only! ... Eating bread and drinking wine will soon remove the illness of the king. Good advice is to be heeded: restlessness, not eating and not drinking disturbs the mind and adds to illness. In this matter the king should listen to his servant.

Modern audiences may feel sympathy with the suffering Esarhaddon. But in a society that saw disease as divine punishment, an ailing king could not expect much compassion. On the contrary, his subjects would see his affliction as an indication that the gods lacked goodwill towards their ruler. Therefore, the king's frailty needed to be concealed. Given the restrictions regulating direct interaction with the monarch, this could be achieved to some extent, but it was essential that Esarhaddon shouldered his manifold public duties as king.

The ancient ritual of the Substitute King was used repeatedly to allow Esarhaddon to escape from the burden of kingship. This ritual was meant to protect the king from mortal danger which was predicted by an eclipse. A substitute took his place for one hundred days. He wore the king's clothes, ate the king's meals, and slept in the king's bed while the true monarch, under the alias 'The Farmer', lived hidden from the public, which given Esarhaddon's desire to do just that was no hardship. Although he was not the only ruler to have the ritual performed, Esarhaddon did so at least four times, which is without parallel. Through references in the private correspondence we can date these instances. One ritual was performed in 671, just eleven days after the first decisive victory of the ongoing Egyptian campaign. While his army continued the war under the Chief Eunuch Aššur-naṣir's command (as an appointment query indicates), Esarhaddon went into hiding. In the following two years, the ritual was performed twice more, allowing Esarhaddon to withdraw for substantial periods. Politically, these absences were perhaps only possible as, in 672, Esarhaddon's son Aššurbanipal had been appointed crown prince of Assyria and subsequently shouldered a significant portion of his father's duties. But Esarhaddon's escape from the throne was not without victims. The ritual directed the predicted evil onto the Substitute King, but this was not left to chance: he was executed at the end of the hundred days. Although a simple mind was normally chosen who would not question his sudden rise to the throne, on at least one occasion Esarhaddon picked a political adversary as Substitute King, in a scheme designed to kill two birds with one stone.

One aspect of his royal duties Esarhaddon fulfilled very well: he fathered many children (at least eighteen). In 670, the first son of his heir Aššurbanipal was born, securing kingship for his descendants into the next two generations. But this same year, a prophecy spread like fire from Harran in northern Syria. A local woman had fallen into ecstasy, uttering a sensational divine message: 'This is the word of (the light god) Nusku: "Kingship belongs to Sasî. I shall destroy the name and the seed of Sennacherib!"' Today, Sasî remains an enigmatic figure whose origins are unknown, but, at the time, he quickly found supporters throughout the empire. The movement to dispose of Esarhaddon was halted promptly but at great cost for the state. According to Esarhaddon's chief physician, the insurrection 'made all other people hateful in the eyes of the king, smearing them like a tanner with the oil of fish', and the Babylonian Chronicles' entry for 670 reads: 'In Assyria, the king killed many of his great ones with the sword.' After the executions in the wake of Sennacherib's murder, this was the second mass culling among the Assyrian state officials that Esarhaddon had ordered within a decade. But the well-oiled machinery of Assyria's administration was the backbone of the empire and these executions caused permanent harm to the state, perhaps more than murdering a king. After all, it had been a testament to the empire's sound administrative structure that the state apparatus could largely absorb the damaging effects of Esarhaddon's frailty and periodic refusal to carry the burden of kingship, while even dramatically expanding the influence of the Assyrian Empire with the conquest of Egypt. In hindsight, the year 670 marks the time when the empire reached its zenith. The second series of executions among the officials greatly weakened the state and brought the expansion of Assyrian power to a grinding halt. Esarhaddon himself died only shortly after in 669, apparently without foul play.

Two scholars of distinguished birth, with frustrated ambitions

The most prominent position for a man of learning was that of the king's principal scholar, called first Royal Scribe (see Chapter 5) and later Master Scholar (*ummānu*). Ever since Gabbu-ilani-ereš had been Master Scholar to kings Tukulti-Ninurta II and Aššurnasirpal II in the 9th century, his family was Assyria's pre-eminent learned clan. Gabbu-ilani-ereš moved with the court from Aššur to the new residence city Kalhu, where his family subsequently flourished. Many of his descendants enjoyed royal patronage as leading experts in the arts of exorcism or in celestial divination, using astrology to predict the future. His descendant Nabu-zuqup-kenu contributed numerous manuscripts of literary and scholarly works to the royal library (see Chapter 6), including a copy of the Gilgameš Epic, and two of his sons served Esarhaddon in very prominent positions. We have already encountered Adad-šumu-uṣur as the king's personal exorcist, trying to coax Esarhaddon out of bouts of depression. His brother Nabu-zeru-lešir was, like their illustrious ancestor, Master Scholar, and as Chief Scribe ultimately responsible for the composition of the king's inscriptions. His son Issar-šumu-ereš succeeded him in this position, continuing his service under King Aššurbanipal. But his other son Šumaya and his nephew Urdu-Gula, who were both trained as exorcists, failed to achieve permanent positions at court. They both wrote petitions to Aššurbanipal that contain detailed descriptions of their economic and social circumstances.

After his father's death had saddled Šumaya with inherited debts, he petitioned crown prince Aššurbanipal twice for financial support and to be assigned some of his father's previous roles. Šumaya used to work for the crown prince and reminded Aššurbanipal in his letters of the family's long association with the royal house, pleading that he should be recognized like his father and grandfather before him. He holds up King Esarhaddon as a role model who would not hesitate to do right by Šumaya—but his attachment, unfortunately, was to Aššurbanipal who was rather less keen to protect this scion of an ancient learned family.

Urdu-Gula, Šumaya's cousin and son of Adad-šumu-uṣur, also found himself excluded from court and cold-shouldered by Aššurbanipal, now king of Assyria. In his emotional petition, Urdu-Gula professed to be bitterly ashamed. With only a small agricultural estate and master of just eight slaves, reduced to wearing old clothes and having to walk ever since his two beasts of burden had died, he was the laughing stock of the scholars who continued to enjoy the king's favour, or so he imagined. He was certainly not a poor man, but his being accustomed to a more affluent situation had led him to incur debts of (at least) three times his former annual income at court. He also despaired over his lack of son and heir and worried who would care for him in old age. He sacrificed to the goddess Ištar of Kadmuri at Kalhu to bless his wife with the desired pregnancy. If this strategy continued to fail, Urdu-Gula would probably have adopted a boy, the usual Assyrian solution to childlessness.

Why did these two men, despite their education, their excellent pedigree, and their familiarity with the royal family, not enjoy a privileged position at court, with all the attached material benefits, that they so obviously thought to be theirs by right? During Esarhaddon's reign, numerous highly qualified scholars joined the king's scholarly entourage from all over the world. Esarhaddon had an Egyptian physician, charged a Babylonian expert with the reorganization of the Babylonian cults, and employed various native experts in specifically Egyptian and Anatolian disciplines of divination and ritual practice. Some of the Assyrian scholars who had grown up expecting to find easy acceptance at court found the competition for the king's favour fiercer than ever before and their ambitions frustrated.

Very rich and friends with the king: a landowner from Dur-Katlimmu

Wealthy landowner Šulmu-šarri was another contemporary of Aššurbanipal. We know about him from the documents excavated in the ruins of his stately home at Dur-Katlimmu (see Chapter 2), the so-called 'Red House' (Figure 9). The archive consists of *c.*150 tablets in Assyrian cuneiform and some fifty triangular clay dockets in alphabetic Aramaic: legal texts that contain much information on the economic situation of Šulmu-šarri's household. That he was an officer in the army is likely, as most people acting as his witnesses in the documents held military titles: Dur-Katlimmu housed a garrison with a chariot corps and intelligence service. When he was at least 50 years of age, Šulmu-šarri was promoted to the distinguished position of a 'Friend' (*ša qurbūte*, literally 'He who is close') of Aššurbanipal, which allowed him to represent the king in confidential matters all over the empire.

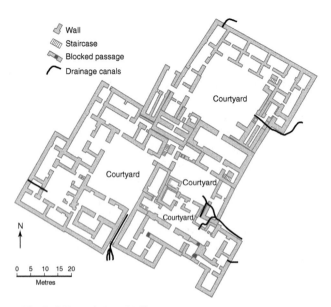

9. The Red House in Dur-Katlimmu.

Like many who enjoyed the king's favour, Šulmu-šarri was a very rich man. His wealth was of an entirely different scale than of well-to-do scholars. The surviving purchase documents alone mention eight fields, three gardens, and three houses and agricultural buildings in and around Dur-Katlimmu, and he also owned an entire village in the region of Aqra in northern Iraq, as we know from a court record dealing with a crime committed there. We can be certain that he had additional estates beyond those mentioned in the documents, some perhaps granted by the king. The 'Red House' is testament to his wealth. With a living space of 5,400 m², this enormous building consists of three separate wings arranged around paved courtyards. The main entrance in the north led into the first part of the building with ample storage facilities, some refrigerated. A central reception hall provided and regulated access to the representative wing in the east and the private quarters in the west of the building. There were two wells, several kitchen areas, and four bathrooms, all connected to the complex sewage system. The building had a second floor, accessible by four staircases. Šulmu-šarri and his family shared this mansion with their many slaves. Within three decades, he bought more than fifty persons. Two-thirds were females, often mothers with young daughters, and the remains of horizontal looms along the walls of the courtyards of the 'Red House' suggest that they contributed to the household's textile production. The shepherds in Šulmu-šarri's employ who grazed their flocks in the steppe east of Dur-Katlimmu provided the necessary wool.

Three adult sons of Šulmu-šarri are attested in the family archive. We do not know anything about their mother, but it is possible that she was a relative, perhaps a sister or daughter, of Šulmu-šarri's close associate Rahimi-il, an officer in the chariot corps. Such a family connection would explain why some of Rahimi-il's legal documents were found in the family archive. The sons inherited their father's estate after he died sometime during the reign of Aššurbanipal's second successor Sin-šarru-iškun, certainly of old age. His grave is not known. Although underground tombs are attested elsewhere in Dur-Katlimmu, no such structure was found at the 'Red House'. Perhaps Šulmu-šarri was buried at another of his many estates.

A wine merchant of Aššur and his customers

Duri-Aššur, head of a trading firm based at Aššur, was another contemporary of King Aššurbanipal. Unlike the scholars Šumaya and Urdu-Gula and the royal 'Friend' Šulmu-šarri, he is unlikely to have been personally acquainted with the king. He lived in the middle of Aššur in a house of $c.150$ m^2 living space. Compared with Šulmu-šarri's gigantic Dur-Katlimmu mansion, this may seem tiny, but in Aššur's densely built-up urban environment, this was a respectable size. The house served as the logistics centre of one of the many private trading companies operating out of Aššur. All its citizens were exempt from taxes, including 'harbour, crossing and gate fees on land or water' and this significantly reduced the cost of importing goods and made trading an attractive enterprise.

The letters and lists excavated in his archive in 1990, 2000, and 2001 during German excavations show that Duri-Aššur and three partners (called 'brothers') organized trade with the northern regions of the Assyrian Empire. He oversaw the logistics of the company in Aššur while his partners travelled to arrange their business activities. The firm employed four caravan leaders who each conducted three trips per year. They travelled upstream along the Tigris with donkeys laden with the silver needed to make the purchases and merchandise from Aššur: hats, shoes, and exclusive textiles, which also served as packing material for supplies and money. Their destination was Zamahu in Jebel Sinjar in the border region between Iraq and Syria, famous for its wines. Once the caravan arrived there, everything was sold, including the donkeys, and Duri-Aššur's agents bought wine with the proceeds, topped up with the silver funds. The wine was filled into animal skins (sheep, goat; rarely cattle). Incidentally, there is a modern link between Assyria and large wine containers, as the nine-litre bottles used for champagne and Burgundy are called 'Salmanazar' (after the French pronunciation of the Assyrian royal name Shalmaneser). The wineskins were bound together with logs to create rafts for the return journey to Aššur on the Tigris. This was good for the wine, as the river kept it cool and prevented it from spoiling. Back in Aššur, all components of the raft constituted valuable merchandise: the wineskins, of course, but also the logs which were much in demand as building timber in forestless Aššur. The wine was subsequently decanted into ceramic vessels similar to amphoras. When served, it was mixed with water. People had (roughly) a pint of wine, sipped from bowls with a volume of just over half a litre. These were balanced elegantly on the fingers of the right hand, which must have impeded overindulgence.

Wine drinking was common among the well-heeled inhabitants of Aššur in the 7th century BC. From the 9th century onwards, the integration of wine-producing regions along the southern flank of the Taurus range into the empire had allowed wine consumption to spread beyond the palace and the temples: wine had long been part of the ritual meals served to the Assyrian gods. For the private consumers in Aššur, wine had to be procured over considerable distances and was an expensive luxury. The solution was to invest in Duri-Aššur's firm, with guaranteed shares of the wine imports in return for silver paid up-front. The firm had a base of loyal customers with repeat investments, who presumably kept their wine cellars well-stocked in this way. Although some investors contributed substantial sums of money, most of the amounts invested were quite small, sometimes just a fraction of a shekel of silver. The investment lists in Duri-Aššur's archive allow a glimpse into the composition of Aššur's wine-loving population in the late 7th century BC: mostly craftsmen and administrative personnel in the service of the temple of Aššur, but also city officials and affiliates of the households of members of the royal family who maintained residences at Aššur. A large number of women invested in the wine firm, and most of them were identified as Egyptian. Egyptian men, too, were among the customers and their presence is not surprising, given that the house right next to Duri-Aššur belonged to an Egyptian family—one of many that settled in the city after the conquest of Memphis in 671 BC. But why did the firm have so many female Egyptian clients? In Egypt, women routinely conducted independent business, unlike in the Assyrian heartland where women could certainly do so, if necessary, but would usually be represented by a male relative. The evidence from Duri-Aššur's archive suggests that even decades after the relocation to Assyria, the Egyptian community still granted their women their traditional independence.

According to their archive, the wine firm was active from 651 until the Medes conquered the city of Aššur in 614 BC; some of Duri-Aššur's letters had not yet been opened when his house went up in flames. The ensuing wars not only terminated the firm's activities but interrupted trans-regional trade on a large scale while the spoils of the Assyrian Empire were divided up between the Babylonian, Median, and Egyptian armies.

Chapter 4
Assyrians abroad

Through the lens of a range of primary sources from different periods, we will capture snapshots of the lives of various Assyrians far away from the city of Aššur and the Assyrian heartland: some happy, some not.

Family matters at the trading colony of Kaneš, c.1900 BC

The Assyrian traders active in Anatolia (see Chapter 2) were far from home, often and for long periods. Those who travelled on business from Aššur were away for at least three months if Kaneš was their destination, and considerably longer if they were on their way to the even more remote Anatolian trading posts such as Durhumit or Purušhaddum. But many lived permanently in Kaneš, or one of the other colonies, as the local representatives of their family firm, sometimes even for several decades. Their families back home in Aššur missed them, as letters excavated in the Assyrian quarter at Kaneš illustrate, especially those from female relatives.

This letter was sent by concerned sisters:

> Here (at Aššur), we have consulted female dream interpreters and diviners and the spirits of the dead: the god Aššur keeps on warning

you! You love money but you hate your life. Can you not satisfy Aššur (here) in the city? As soon as you read this letter, come here to see the eye of Aššur and (thus) save your life.

The records of the family firm show that when the brother returned to Aššur after many years abroad, it was with sadly depleted funds. Once in a while, female family members made the trip to Anatolia but a male relative needed to chaperon them. As a mother from Aššur wrote to her son in Kaneš:

Come quickly (to Aššur) so that I can depart with you and watch over your father's and your house (i.e. the family firm) in Kaneš so that no one will make trouble for your father's house.

It would seem that the father was in a frail state of health and did not have long to live. Earlier in the same letter, the mother reminded the son of his obligations to his family:

If not you, who else do we have over there (in Kaneš)? If not you, your father has nobody else over there! Act like a man, heed your father's instructions, keep your father's documents safe and ask all his outstanding claims to be paid. Sell your father's merchandise, then get ready and come here (to Aššur) so that you may see the eye of the god Aššur and of your father and thus please your father!

Some wives followed their merchant husbands through Anatolia— not necessarily a recipe for harmony and happiness, if one consults one wife's letter chronicling the stations of her life in Anatolia and the increasingly dysfunctional relationship with her husband who was most of the time in another place and treated her shabbily when they were together. The wife wrote the following, after she found herself once again abandoned, this time in the trading colony at Hahhum (near Samsat in Turkey):

You left me in Purušhaddum and I really was wiped from my husband's mind. (Now) you do not take care of me when I have come here (to Hahhum)! In Kaneš, you degraded me and for a whole year would not let me come to your bed. From Timilkiya you wrote to me: 'If you don't come here you are no longer my wife! I will make it even worse than in Purušhaddum.' Then you went from Timilkiya to Kaneš, saying: 'I will leave again (from Kaneš) within 15 days,' but instead of 15 days you stayed there for a year! You wrote to me from Kaneš: 'Come up to Hahhum.' So now I have been living in Hahhum for a year and you do not even mention my name in your business letters!

No wonder most wives stayed behind in Aššur.

During their residency in Kaneš, some Assyrian residents married local women and started another family there despite the fact that they already had wife and children back home. Such an arrangement was perfectly above board, as long as the two women did not live in the same city: only one was considered the 'wife' (*aššatum*), usually the one residing in Aššur, while the other was merely a consort and designated as *amtum:* this word elsewhere means 'slave woman' in Assyrian but in this specific context stands for secondary local wife. Bigamy was not otherwise practised in Kaneš and the records of local families indicate that the native inhabitants were monogamous. But an exception was made, and gladly, when the groom was a prosperous Assyrian trader and an attractive catch on the marriage market.

A few houses inhabited by local Anatolian families yielded archives of cuneiform tablets, mostly legal texts documenting debts and purchases. The extensive correspondences that are characteristic for the Assyrian archives are missing—unsurprising, given that there was no need to maintain long-distance relationships with family and business associates abroad. Interestingly, the inhabitants of Kaneš did not adapt the cuneiform script to Hittite, their spoken language: deliberately, it seems, as it would have been perfectly possible to do so, as the many loanwords and names in the Assyrian-language tablets demonstrate. Instead, they preferred to write in Assyrian even within their own community, and this is in line with the high regard in evidence for all things Assyrian.

Regardless of their social standing in Aššur, traders who married local girls generally seem to have had their pick from among the wealthiest local families, even though the Kaneš-born spouse had to accept being in a lopsided relationship that favoured the Assyrian husband. In a marriage between locals, on the other hand, husband and wife would have been equals and owned all property jointly. But perhaps this imbalance was offset by the fact that mixed marriage was not 'till death do us part'. Instead, such a relationship had an expiry date, the husband's permanent departure to Aššur, when a divorce contract was drawn up that typically left the woman with the house in Kaneš, a certain sum of money, and the freedom to remarry. While the Assyrian father might choose to take some of the children to Aššur, he had to provide for the upbringing of those who remained in Kaneš with their mother. The prospect of future financial gain clearly eclipsed any concerns that the local women's families might otherwise have entertained regarding the suitability of the arrangement.

Envoys to Pharaoh Akhenaten's court, c.1340 BC

Pharaoh Thutmose III (15th century BC; 18th Dynasty) greatly expanded Egyptian power by leading military campaigns deep into Syria and even reached the Euphrates, to him 'that inverted water which goes downstream in going upstream'. He established a border with Mittani and on three occasions accepted gifts from the rulers under its authority, including the unnamed leader of Aššur. This was most likely Aššur-nadin-ahhe I who, if we can believe one of his successors, had at one point received twenty talents of gold from Egypt. The actual sum may have substantially increased in Assyrian memory in the intervening century or else Aššur-uballit I, who quoted this figure, may have deliberately inflated the amount in order to shame his correspondent Pharaoh Akhenaten into sending a similarly generous gift; after all, his former overlord, the king of Mittani (Hanigalbat to the Assyrians), also had received twenty talents. But however that may be, Egypt's gold certainly captured the Assyrian ruler's imagination and emerges from the sources as a key incentive for diplomatic contact with the far-away kingdom on the Nile.

Aššur-uballit I was the first Assyrian ruler to adopt the titles of a king and, during his rule of over three decades, he proved extremely successful in establishing his brand-new kingdom as a powerful state. Towards the end of his reign, he even marched on Babylon in order to install a king acceptable to him (see Chapter 5). The two letters found among the state correspondence of the pharaohs of the later 18th Dynasty of Egypt, dubbed the 'Amarna Letters' after their findspot, date from earlier in his reign. He appears to have not yet fully undergone the metamorphosis from local ruler to international statesman. The first of his letters was composed in Assyrian and is quite short, especially if one considers that it had to be transported over a vast distance to reach its recipient. From Aššur, the envoy carrying the letter had to cross all of Syria, and then travel down the Mediterranean Coast. Skirting the Sinai Peninsula along the coastal route, he would then have reached the Delta of the Nile and continued upstream to the capital of Akhetaten, modern Amarna. In total, this is a distance of 1,450 kilometres, as the crow flies, but overland of at least 1,800 kilometres.

Aššur-uballit's envoy brought with him a greeting gift, which would have been officially presented once he secured an audience with the pharaoh. In his first diplomatic overture, the Assyrian king sent a chariot and two horses as well as a lump of lapis lazuli, a highly prized precious stone of dark blue colour from faraway Afghanistan. Apart from initiating contact, the first letter of Aššur-uballit was mostly concerned with making sure that his envoy would return promptly:

Do not delay the envoy whom I sent to you for a visit. He should
visit and then leave for here. He should see what you are like and
what your country is like, and then leave for here.

The second letter is perhaps more polished in style but not very
different in tone. It was not written in Assyrian but in Babylonian,
the language of international politics. It was also much longer.
Aššur-uballit and his chancellery had been researching past
dealings with Egypt and, as we have seen, peppered the letter with
facts and figures in a bid to secure a suitable gift in return for the
Assyrian offering: a chariot with two white horses fit for a king,
another chariot, and a lapis lazuli seal. The Assyrian king stated
very clearly what he wanted as a return gift: gold, and ideally
more than he had received before.

Gold in your country is dust; one simply gathers it up. Why are you
so sparing of it? I am engaged with building a new palace. Send me
as much gold as is needed for its adornment.

And the letter continued:

We are countries far apart. Are our messengers to be always on the
march for such (poor) results?

For fledgling statesman Aššur-uballit, diplomatic contact with
Egypt may have been mainly about the money, but he was truly
pleased that Akhenaten had sent a delegation for a return visit to
Aššur. Although he had insisted that his own envoy should be sent
back immediately, he had no such intentions:

When I saw your envoys, I was very happy. Certainly your envoys
shall reside with me, held in great esteem.

Showing off Egyptian diplomats to the Assyrian elite and to
visiting dignitaries was bound to raise Aššur-uballit's prestige.

His own envoy remains anonymous in the available sources, but he was certainly a high-ranking individual, and perhaps a member of the royal family. The Hittite envoy Teli-Šarruma who was dispatched to the court of Tukulti-Ninurta I of Assyria in the 13th century, for example, was a prince. He is attested as one of a group of diplomats visiting Assyria in texts from Harbe (modern Tell Chuera in north-east Syria). Teli-Šarruma travelled with four teams of horses, three teams of mules and six donkeys, having delivered letters and gifts to the city of Aššur, as had the envoy of the Syrian state of Amurru who took the trip with ten donkeys. The Phoenician envoy from Sidon in Lebanon travelled much lighter, with just a chariot and three donkeys, but he had only letters to deliver, albeit important ones sent from the Egyptian pharaoh to the Assyrian king. All envoys, their staff and their animals were guaranteed board and lodging. The documents excavated at Harbe arranged for the delegations' provisioning at each stop on their way back home, as long as they were in Assyrian territory. For Aššur-uballit's envoy travelling from Aššur to Akhetaten a century earlier, the situation will have been similar.

Banished to the mountains, c. 1082 BC

Palaeoclimatologists explore past climatic conditions by analysing materials whose properties were influenced by the surrounding climate in order to recover proxy data. Two approaches work well for the ancient Middle East. The first method uses a very big drill to recover ancient sediments, preferably from the bottom of lakes ('lake cores'), and collect pollen and other climate indicators in order to measure temperature, oxygen content, and nutrient levels, as well as charcoal in order to date the layers through carbon dating. The other method uses a much smaller drill to cut into karst cave formations (speleothems) to recover sequences of the microscopic layers, added annually as water drips down and whose chemical properties differ each year. The resulting analyses show that around 1200 BC, a period of comparative cool with associated increased rainfalls came to an end, having lasted for about three centuries. Subsequently, climatic conditions warmed up and there was less rain: this more arid period lasted until *c*.900 BC. The drier climate was bad news for marginal farming regions because it made rain-fed agriculture, as traditionally practised in northern Mesopotamia, a hazardous gamble.

In 1987 climatologist Jehuda Neumann and assyriologist Simo Parpola had already proposed a connection between the climate shift and the mass migrations that destabilized much of the Middle East at the time. In particular, Parpola refined the understanding of a long-known but fragmentary Assyrian chronicle text, that gives the following entry for the year 1082 BC:

[In King Tiglath-pileser I's 32nd year, a famine occurred so severe that] people ate one another's flesh; [...] Aramean 'houses' plundered [the land], seized the roads, and conquered and took [many fortified cities] of Assyria. [The people of Assyria fled] to the mountains of Habriuri [to save their] lives. [The Arameans] took their [houses?], their money and their property.

The chronicle text uses the spectre of cannibalism to indicate that the food shortage was so bad that social order collapsed. The same image is used elsewhere, for example in the inscriptions of King Aššurbanipal in accounts about the consequences of the Babylonian insurrection led by his brother Šamaš-šumu-ukin from 652 to 648 BC. However, the 1082 BC famine did not happen in Assyria but elsewhere, triggering an Aramean invasion that was not simply a raid for food but an effort to claim land. The specific setting for the events recorded in the chronicle was the valley of the Upper Zab, as the region of Habriuri can be identified with the high plain of Herir, east of Arbela in the western flanks of the Zagros. This was where the Assyrians fled to from the Aramean invaders, its mountain location promising safety as well as relatively stable economic conditions. But subsequently,

Habriuri too was lost to Assyrian control. In the mid-10th century, King Aššur-dan II made efforts to regain the region and sacked several settlements there, as reported in his inscriptions. Also,

> I brought back the exhausted [people] of Assyria who had
> abandoned [their cities and houses because of] want, hunger, and
> famine and [had gone up] to other lands. [I settled] them in
> [suitable] cities and houses and they dwelt in peace.

Assyrian control of Habriuri was imposed for good when Aššurnasirpal II established an Assyrian province there in 883 BC.

Similar events to these took place elsewhere in the realm at the beginning and the end of the dry spell. A private legal document from Dunnu-ša-Uzibi (modern Giricano near Diyarbakir in south-eastern Turkey) dates to the year 1069 or 1068 BC and highlights the weakening of Assyrian control in the Upper Tigris region at a time when the Arameans were attacking the area according to a royal inscription of King Aššur-bel-kala. According to the legal document, a man had entered into a commercial partnership to finance a business trip. A unique clause not known from any other contract protected his partner's investment, should the man 'flee into the mountains': the partner could then claim his estate's next harvest. Again it was only Aššurnasirpal II who was able to reclaim the region for Assyria in 882. He relocated the people to the settlements that had been abandoned a few generations earlier for the highlands of Šubria, the mountainous region to the north of the Upper Tigris valley, quite similar in character to Habriuri. Using the same language as his great-grandfather Aššur-dan II for the Assyrians of Habriuri, his inscription reads:

> I brought back the exhausted people of Assyria who had gone up to
> other lands, to the mountains of Šubria, because of famine and
> hunger and I settled them in the city of Tušhan.

From these sources, it appears that the Assyrian territories on the Upper Zab and on the Upper Tigris, as well as on the Khabur and the Euphrates, were lost to the kingdom. It was not because the more arid conditions failed the large-scale agriculture there; but these economically relatively stable lowlands attracted hungry Aramean clans, called 'houses' and typically named after a founding father, such as Bit-Aduni, 'House of Aduni'. The Arameans had previously settled in more marginal regions such as Jebel Bishri in Central Syria where farming had been possible during the colder, wetter period from *c.*1500 to 1200 BC. Now, they sought out territories with a more secure economic basis and settled there, each 'house' developing into a small regional state. The local Assyrian population was forced to move to higher altitudes. How keen they were to be brought 'back home' into the realm from the mid-10th century onwards is open for discussion. But from the point of view of the Assyrian government, the need to rescue these enclave populations, routinely described as 'exhausted', provided a welcome reason for beginning a war of liberation against the Aramean houses that had in the meantime established themselves as small regional states.

An unpopular ambassador, *c.*710 BC

By the late 8th century, the Assyrian Empire controlled regions organized in around sixty-five provinces, run by governors who were appointed by the king. In those regions that accepted Assyrian authority but remained client states under the control of local governments, ambassadors ('Trusted Ones' in Assyrian) represented the empire's interests. Like the governors, they routinely communicated with the king through letters and envoys.

One such client state was Kumme. Like many polities that were allowed to keep their nominal independence, this small mountain kingdom occupied a location that impeded direct Assyrian control. Whereas the Phoenician states of Tyre and Arwad were protected by their island location off the Mediterranean coast,

Kumme was located north of the Iraqi–Turkish border in the upper reaches of the Lesser Khabur, in the region of modern Beytüşşebap. Kumme was an ancient city-state with a temple dedicated to the storm god. Beytüşşebap boasts a hot thermal spring whose water is said to cure various ailments, and the spring alone would have recommended the site as a major sanctuary. Moreover, the dramatic mountain landscape provided the setting for myths about the storm god's battles against such foes as the rock monster Ullikummi; the avalanches and landslides that occur frequently in the region were seen as a manifestation of the god's power. His shrine had since the early second millennium BC attracted royal patronage from far away, including Mari in Syria, Hattuša in Central Anatolia, and also Assyria; King Adad-nerari II sacrificed at the shrine in 895. In 879 delegates from Kumme celebrated the inauguration of the imperial centre Kalhu as the guests of Aššurnasirpal II.

After Tiglath-pileser III had conquered the nearby kingdom of Ullubu in 739 BC, Kumme's territory bordered directly onto the newly established Assyrian province of Birtu. But at first the empire made no attempt to incorporate the tiny state. The correspondence of Sargon II provides us with much information on the relationship between Assyria and its client state, which remained under the control of its native ruler. At the time (c.710 BC) Ariye was city lord of Kumme. He was bound to the empire by treaty and in return for Assyria's protection had to accept certain obligations: to supply manpower, horses, and timber; and to provide intelligence on the region. For this purpose, Kumme was excellently positioned, as it was located on the direct, if difficult mountain route leading from Assyria's heartland to the centre of Urartu on Lake Van in eastern Turkey. Despite its links to Assyria, Kumme entertained close relations with Urartu, even providing it with men and information. This did not happen behind Assyria's back but with its encouragement and support, as it was considered a good way of gaining access to intelligence about the arch enemy.

A key strategy in ensuring Kumme's loyalty to Assyria was the permanent presence of an ambassador at Ariye's court. This position was held by Aššur-reṣuwa, whose letters to Sargon constitute the most extensive surviving dossier of any Assyrian ambassador. His messages frequently describe routine affairs such as timber transports. But they also concern Assyrian–Urartian espionage and counterespionage, thrilling to read even millennia after the events. Most exciting, perhaps, is to learn about the last-minute disclosure of an Urartian plan to abduct several Assyrian governors from Kumme's territory. Crown prince Sennacherib reports to his father, quoting Ariye's report on his neighbour, the ruler of Ukku, who was conspiring with Urartu:

> The ruler of Ukku has written to the Urartian king that the governors of the king of Assyria are building a fort in Kumme, and the Urartian king has given his governors the following order: 'Take your troops, go and capture the governors of the king of Assyria alive from the Kummeans, and bring them to me.' I do not have the full details yet; as soon as I have heard more, I shall write by express to the crown prince that they should rush troops to me.

For Kumme, this plot seems to have resulted in a significant tightening of Assyrian control. When sometime after 714 BC the new king of Urartu questioned the absence of Kummean delegates at his court, the answer from Kumme, according to the information conveyed back to Sargon, was this:

> Since we are subjects of Assyria, a cavalry foreman is our superior. Only the houses of Kumme are left to us; … we cannot put our feet anywhere.

Kumme was now firmly under the thumb of the Assyrian military. While city lord Ariye and his son Arizâ, who are both mentioned in this letter, seem to have been loyal to Assyria, not everyone in Kumme shared their zeal. Aššur-reṣuwa, like all ambassadors serving in the Assyrian client states, had unlimited access to Kumme's ruler and influenced his decisions openly. The privileges of these officials are sketched in one of the few bilateral Assyrian treaties to survive in the original, the 676 BC agreement between Esarhaddon and the king of Tyre. A fragmentary passage outlines how the client ruler had to interact with the Assyrian ambassador:

> [When] the elders of your country [convene to take] counsel the ambassador [must be] with them.... [If...], do not listen to him, [do not...] without the ambassador. Nor must you open a letter that I send to you without the ambassador. If the ambassador is absent, wait for him and then open it.

Not surprisingly, many Kummeans perceived ambassador Aššur-reṣuwa's activities as oppressive and invasive. He in turn identified several people as dangerous to the Assyrian interests, writing to his king:

> There are four men who should be removed. They must not walk free in my presence while I am here. They are inciting the country.

Aššur-reṣuwa became so unpopular that the people of Kumme petitioned Sargon and others to recall him from his post, protesting that while he was utterly loathsome they were still loyal to the empire. Hence in a letter to the king from another official,

> The Kummeans who previously appealed to the king, my lord, have returned and come to me, saying: 'Kumme in its entirety cannot stand the ambassador. But we can and will bear the responsibility (towards the empire)'.

Another letter, however, reveals that the city lord's standing had been affected by the hatred for the Assyrian ambassador:

> Now then Kumme in its entirety has turned against Ariye; they [...] and speak of killing [the ambassador].

How this particular situation ended for the ambassador Aššur-reṣuwa personally is unknown. But crucially, a client ruler who had lost his ability to lead his country was worthless to the empire.

The available sources do not reveal whether these sentiments gave way to an attempt to oust Ariye but similar events happened repeatedly in the client states. Time and again, their own subjects unseated pro-Assyrian rulers and instead backed other pretenders who would not accept Assyria's supremacy. This usually led to a quick Assyrian intervention and quite frequently to the annexation of the state in question. Action against those representing Assyria, whether ambassador or native ruler, whether only planned or implemented, was enough to bring Kummean independence to an end, and not even the Assyrian appreciation for the famous temple of the storm-god would have changed that. The city-state disappears from the sources and we can assume that the tiny mountain realm became part of the Assyrian province of Birtu. The maintenance of a cordon of buffer states against Urartu was advantageous for the Assyrian Empire, but if the mechanisms of indirect control were not respected in the client states, the next best solution was to simply do away with local government altogether.

Sibling rivalry: Šamaš-šumu-ukin, king of Babylon, 648 BC

In 672 Aššurbanipal was elevated to the rank of crown prince of Assyria, and at the same time, his older brother Šamaš-šumu-ukin was declared crown prince of Babylon. Their father Esarhaddon himself ruled as king of Assyria and Babylon but wanted to see the southern territory under separate government. As he put it in an inscription:

> I gave Šamaš-šumu-ukin, my son and offspring, as a present to the god Marduk and the goddess Zarpanitu.

The whole empire had to swear to respect and honour the king's decision to appoint his sons Aššurbanipal and Šamaš-šumu-ukin as his successors, with governors and client rulers taking an oath on behalf of their subjects. The text of the loyalty treaty was inscribed on large clay tablets that were sealed with the three sacred seals of the god Aššur. The first was created in the 19th century, the second in the 13th century, and the last c.700 BC. About 200 copies must have been written and distributed at the time, and 10 manuscripts have been found in Aššur (a fragment only), Kalhu (8 copies), and most recently Kullania (Tell Tayinat in the Hatay region of Turkey), where a Canadian team led by Tim Harrison unearthed the copy of the governor of Kullania inside the cella of a small shrine in 2008. It was apparently displayed there as a divine icon, following the treaty's instructions:

> You shall guard this covenant tablet which is sealed with the seal of the god Aššur, king of the gods, and set it up in your presence, like your own god.

Esarhaddon's new succession arrangements were disseminated throughout the empire, also expressed by visual means. Assyrian royal steles usually show only the king. But Esarhaddon had steles erected in Sam'al (Zinjirli, also located in the Hatay; see Figure 8) and Til-Barsip (Tell Ahmar in Syria) that depict himself on the front and, in smaller scale, the two crown princes on the left and right-hand sides of the stele. Šamaš-šumu-ukin is shown wearing the traditional Babylonian royal garments. Also the image displayed on the royal seal was adapted to fit the new situation and to promote the succession arrangements. While the traditional depiction showed the king killing a lion the updated design repeated this subject three times (Figure 10). All this conveys that Esarhaddon and the princes were to govern the empire jointly, and contemporary letters indeed show both princes involved in matters of political and cultic importance.

10. Impression of a stamp seal with three depictions of the king fighting a rampant lion, the emblem of Assyrian kingship. From Nineveh.

When Esarhaddon died in 669, Aššurbanipal ascended to the Assyrian throne, and Šamaš-šumu-ukin became king of Babylon, as planned. But their relationship quickly soured as the Assyrian king thought himself the overlord and his brother a mere client ruler. A host of Babylonian officials reported directly to Aššurbanipal who also controlled Babylonia's foreign affairs; there was no separate army either. At some point, Aššurbanipal even claimed publicly that it was he who had installed the king of Babylon. Šamaš-šumu-ukin made a bid to break free of the embrace of brother and empire in 652. We do not know what prompted him. Had he gone native after nearly two decades in the south? But it is clear that not everyone in Babylonia supported this bid for independence. The country was deeply divided between Assyrian loyalists and a Babylonian faction that, somewhat perversely, followed an Assyrian. The Iranian kingdom of Elam and the leaders of the southern Aramean tribes supported Šamaš-šumu-ukin and provided badly needed military assistance. In turn, Aššurbanipal sent his army south.

Four years of bloody war followed, documented in a number of letters from the Assyrian state correspondence as well as Aššurbanipal's inscriptions. The conflict greatly destabilized Babylonia and led to severe famines, especially in those cities put under siege. People were forced to abandon their children, selling them for extremely little money at a time when prices for food were skyrocketing. Legal texts include clauses that specifically reference this in order to protect the buyer from future claims. The Assyrian side eventually emerged victorious but at great cost for Babylonia and for the entire empire. Šamaš-šumu-ukin's rebellion had severely damaged the credibility of Assyrian imperial sovereignty; other client states dared to push their luck and some, like Egypt, slipped out of the empire's hold.

Aššurbanipal and Šamaš-šumu-ukin had an older sister, Šerua-etirat, who had occupied a prominent position at her father's court, as documented in various letters. She tried to mediate in the conflict between her royal brothers. This is not known from contemporary sources but from a later literary composition about the conflict, recorded in Aramaic language and Demotic script on an Egyptian papyrus of the 4th century BC. In this story, Šerua-etirat appears firmly in Aššurbanipal's camp. She pleads with Šamaš-šumu-ukin to reconcile with the brother, but fails to convince him. She then suggests that he should kill himself together with his children and, interestingly, his scholars whom she blames for his unreasonableness. After all, they had filled his head with ideas about Babylonian kingship that were directly responsible for the present crisis. Says Šerua-etirat in the story:

> If you will not listen to my words and if you will not pay attention to my speech, leave the house of (god) Bel, go away from the house of

(god) Marduk. Let there be built for you a house of [...] construct a house of [...]. Throw down tar and pitch and sweet smelling perfumes. Bring in your sons and daughters and your scholars who have made you arrogant. When you see how (low) they have sunk to your detriment, let fire burn your fat with (that of) your sons and daughters and your scholars who have made you arrogant.

Šerua-etirat's suggestion for her brother to construct a funeral pyre and then burn himself, his children, and the scholars can be connected with Šamaš-šumu-ukin's death in a fire, as recorded in the inscriptions of Aššurbanipal.

This story, dubbed today The Tale of Two Brothers, is one of several Aramaic compositions that appraise 7th century Assyrian palace life. The Tale of the Sage Ahiqar is another example. It is known from a 5th century BC papyrus found in Elephantine in southern Egypt and deals with a scholar in Sennacherib's and Esarhaddon's service. Both tales draw on historical events and feature some accurate insider information, suggesting that they originated in the palace milieu. That such literature was composed in Aramaic highlights how widely spoken and used this language was even at court. That these stories are still transmitted centuries later, and in Egypt, demonstrates the lasting fascination of the cosmopolitan Assyrian imperial court culture.

Chapter 5
Foreigners in Assyria

This chapter looks at Assyrian interactions with the wider world by focusing on foreigners in the city of Aššur and how they got there. The first two cases explore Assyrian political and cultural links to the Mesopotamian south in the second millennium BC. The third case shows Assyrian diplomacy in action when an Anatolian ruler was invited, like it or not, to visit Aššur. The last two cases focus on inhabitants of the city of Aššur who had been relocated there by force from Iran and serve to emphasize how the Assyrian heartland was an increasingly multicultural, cosmopolitan environment during its imperial phase.

Role model: Samsi-Addu, conqueror of Aššur, 18th century BC

Although he did not originate from the city, King Samsi-Addu ruled over Aššur for thirty-three years during the 18th century BC, having subjugated it in the course of his extended wars of conquest. So successful were his victories that he claimed the title 'King of the Universe'. While Aššur was a valuable addition to his growing realm, he did not take up residence there but installed his elder son as regent over the city; Išme-Dagan resided in nearby Ekallate. The city and its god, however, were important enough to Samsi-Addu to merit his special attention. He rebuilt the god

Aššur's sanctuary and added a monumental stepped tower in the southern Mesopotamian tradition to the temple complex. The remains of his building works were unearthed during Walter Andrae's excavations in Aššur, which also yielded copies of the inscription celebrating this effort.

The Assyrian kings Shalmaneser I in the 13th century BC and Esarhaddon in the 7th century prominently referenced him, as Šamši-Adad under the Assyrianized version of his West-Semitic name, when describing the building history of the Aššur temple prior to their own renovation projects. In doing so, they also honoured his request as expressed in the inscription:

> When the temple becomes dilapidated, may whoever among the kings, my sons, renovate the temple anoint my clay and stone inscriptions with oil, make sacrifices and return them to their paces.

Assyrian rulers habitually looked for the foundation documents of their predecessors and deposited them with their own. This is the relevant passage in Esarhaddon's inscription from the Aššur temple:

> The earlier temple of the god Aššur, which Ušpia, my ancestor, regent of the god Aššur, had first built, became dilapidated and Erišum (I), son of Ilu-šuma, my ancestor, priest of the god Aššur, rebuilt it. 126 years passed and it became dilapidated again, and Šamši-Adad (I), son of Ilu-kabkabi, my ancestor, regent of the god Aššur, rebuilt it. 434 years passed and that temple was destroyed in a fire, (and) Shalmaneser (I), son of Adad-nerari (I), my ancestor, regent of the god Aššur, rebuilt it. 580 years passed and the inner cella, the residence of the god Aššur, my lord,…became dilapidated, aged, and antiquated. I was worried, afraid, and hesitant about renovating that temple. In the diviner's bowl, the gods Šamaš and Adad answered me with a firm 'yes' and they had (their response) concerning the rebuilding of that temple and the renovation of its chapel written on a liver.

The last passage refers to the sacrificial divination (see Chapter 3) undertaken to confirm that the gods indeed supported the intended building project.

In Samsi-Addu's inscription for the Aššur temple, the god is called Enlil, after the great southern Mesopotamian god. Aššur was seemingly taken to be but a facet of that deity as whose protégé Samsi-Addu described himself here and elsewhere. Šubat-Enlil 'Seat of Enlil' was the name that the king gave to the capital city that he created for his newly forged realm at Tell Leilan in the Khabur Triangle region of north-eastern Syria. In his own words of the Aššur temple inscription, he was the one 'who combined the land between Tigris and Euphrates'. The 18th century BC was in general a period marked by the formation of large trans-regional polities in the Middle East. At that time, for example, the rulers of Kaneš created a territorial state in central Anatolia that was the first incarnation of the so-called Hittite kingdom. The changed geopolitical situation was bad news for the merchant firms from Aššur as the additional costs enforced by the powerful new states cut deeply into their profit margins. Eventually, they abandoned their trading colonies in Anatolia altogether.

Towards the end of his long reign, Samsi-Addu expanded his power beyond the Tigris as far as the western flanks of the Zagros mountains and conquered regions that later constituted the Assyrian heartland. The extent of his realm therefore anticipated the borders of the kingdom of Assyria in the 13th century BC. But it was a fleeting creation that did not outlast its creator and quickly disintegrated after his death. The city of Aššur remained under the authority of his son Išme-Dagan, but he had to rely on allies in the south for his political survival and three times even fled to the city of Babylon. Soon after his death, Aššur reverted to local rule.

While the later rulers of the kingdom of Assyria habitually refer to Samsi-Addu as their ancestor, the immediate successors of his short-lived dynasty begged to differ. Thus we read in an inscription of Puzur-Sin:

> By the command of the god Aššur, my lord, I destroyed that
> improper thing which he had worked on: the wall and the palace of
> Šamši-Adad, his grandfather—a foreign plague, not of the flesh of
> the city of Aššur, who had destroyed the shrines of the city of Aššur.

Earlier in the inscription, the grandson is identified:

> When I, Puzur-Sin, regent of the god Aššur, son of Aššur-bel-šamê,
> destroyed the evil of Asinum, offspring of Šamši-[Adad], ... and
> reinstituted proper rule for the city of Aššur.

The text creates an opposition between good and evil, between Assyrian and foreign, between Samsi-Addu's fortifications and palace and the city's temples. The conqueror, his heirs, and what they had created are rejected wholesale.

Samsi-Addu was indeed a foreigner whose rule over Aššur was not a birthright but the prize of conquest. Already the close relationship claimed with the god Enlil suggests his southern origin. Moreover, the list of his ancestors corresponds to the genealogy of another ruler who forged himself a large realm by conquest. Hammurabi, king of Babylon, is today best known for the monumental stele whose inscription includes a long list of legal rulings to demonstrate that he was the 'King of Justice': the so-called Code of Hammurabi. He and Samsi-Addu are likely to have been members of the same clan. The roots of the conqueror of Aššur are therefore today sought in the region of modern Baghdad where the Diyala flows into the Tigris.

Despite his non-Assyrian origins, Samsi-Addu was featured prominently in the so-called Assyrian King List, a document that records the rulers of Aššur and the length of their reigns. It incorporated not only Samsi-Addu and his son Išme-Dagan into the list of native rulers, but also their (and Hammurabi's) ancestors who had never even set foot into the city. Was this an attempt to legitimize Samsi-Addu's rule over Aššur by muddling his origins, or were the famous 'King of the Universe' and his ancestors claimed by the later Assyrian rulers as prestigious forefathers? Modern opinions are divided, and much depends on how the editorial history of the Assyrian King List is reconstructed. Neither Samsi-Addu's last heir, Asinum, nor Puzur-Sin, who ushered in a period of restoration after the end of Samsi-Addu's dynasty at Aššur, were included in the composition. This suggests that the text was compiled only at a later date when it was considered again more opportune to integrate Samsi-Addu smoothly into Assyrian history. However that may be, the resultant text was subsequently subject to periodic updating as entries for each Assyrian ruler were added. The text survives in several manuscripts, the latest written at the time of Shalmaneser V at the end of the 8th century BC. It is a key source for the reconstruction of the chronology of the entire ancient Middle East.

At the very least, by the 13th century BC, when King Shalmaneser I mentioned Samsi-Addu's renovation of the Aššur temple in his own building account, the conqueror was unreservedly understood as an Assyrian ruler and direct ancestor of the present king. At that time, no one desired to eradicate the memory or the physical traces of Samsi-Addu's rule over Aššur. As the previous master of a vast realm, the illustrious predecessor now served as a role model for the kings of Assyria and to mark this, they adopted his titles 'Appointee of the God Enlil' and the programmatic 'King of the Universe'.

Marduk-nadin-ahhe, Royal Scribe from Babylon, c.1328 BC

Peace with Babylonia was important to Aššur-uballit I, the first king of Assyria in the 14th century BC. According to Babylonian chronicle texts, he secured good relations with the southern neighbour by marrying his daughter Muballitat-Šerua to Burnaburiaš

II, king of Babylon. Their son (Aššur-uballit's grandson) would inherit the Babylonian crown. However, when Burnaburiaš died in 1328 BC, the Babylonians turned against their new ruler Karahardaš, executed him and replaced him with Nazibugaš, the 'Son of a Nobody', that is, a person not related to the royal family. Why this happened is unknown, but as the slain king's royal grandfather Aššur-uballit immediately invaded Babylonia, it may have been precisely Karahardaš's Assyrian connections that had been the cause of his unpopularity. The Assyrian army made short work of the usurper, who was killed. Aššur-uballit claimed the throne for Kurigalzu II, another of his grandsons.

The loyalties of the Babylonians must have been divided between the rebels backing Nazibugaš and the supporters of the legitimate royal house. One man who may have been caught up in the conflict was the scribe Marduk-nadin-ahhe, a member of a distinguished family that had served the Babylonian rulers for several generations in high administrative and scholarly offices. This man chose to leave Babylonia and found a new home at the Assyrian capital of Aššur where he took up the distinguished position of Aššur-uballit's Royal Scribe. This office seems to correspond to the later title of Master Scholar (see Chapter 3) and presumably the incumbent fulfilled similar duties towards his kingly patron, composing royal inscriptions and other official texts, advising the monarch in scholarly matters, and perhaps even tutoring members of the royal family in scribal lore. Marduk-nadin-ahhe is the earliest Royal Scribe attested at the Assyrian court and presumably the office was created at that time. Aššur-uballit's mission was to confirm his kingdom of Assyria, until recently subordinate to Mittani, as a great realm. Establishing a highly visible role for a scholarly adviser to the king fits this objective very well, especially if the newly appointed Royal Scribe was descended from a family whose members had served the Babylonian crown in this fashion.

What we know about Marduk-nadin-ahhe derives from an inscription that he composed on the occasion of moving into his new house in Aššur. The text, known only from a later copy, concludes with appeals to the god Marduk, the lord of Babylon, for whom a shrine had been erected in the crowded temple quarter of Aššur during the reign of Aššur-uballit:

> May the god Marduk, my lord, inspect that house, and grant (it) to me for my troubles. May he allow (it) to endure in the future for my sons, my grandsons, my offspring, and the offspring of my offspring, so that we, I and my family, can revere Marduk, my lord, and Zarpanitu, my lady, forever, and perhaps, by the command of Marduk, someone can set straight my [relatives] and ancestral clan that have embraced treachery. May [Marduk], my lord, grant to Aššur-uballit, who loves me, king of the universe, my lord, long days with abundant prosperity.

From the unusual references to his troubles and to treacherous family members, it emerges quite clearly that Marduk-nadin-ahhe had been caught up in conflict in Babylonia prior to finding a new home under his patron and benefactor Aššur-uballit at Aššur, where he permanently hoped to establish himself and his family. He clearly did not contemplate that he or his descendants would ever return to his native Babylon.

The exile built his house from scratch next to the Marduk shrine, certainly with royal blessing, as living space in the cramped city of Aššur was at a premium and constructing a new house in the temple quarter would have required clearing away the existing buildings. The Divine Directory of Aššur (see Chapter 2) would seem to suggest that the Marduk shrine was part of the extended Aššur temple complex, and this would mean that Marduk-nadin-ahhe's house, 'erected in the shadow of the temple of Marduk', was built very close-by or perhaps even inside it. This would imply a priestly function for the Babylonian, most likely in the service of the cult of Marduk and his consort Zarpanitu.

Regardless of its location, with two wings, one accessible to the public, the other private living space with an underground tomb underneath the innermost room, the house conforms to the typical standards of an elite residence in Aššur, and even had its own well. The first part of the inscription reads:

> I, Marduk-nadin-ahhe, royal scribe, son of Marduk-uballit, son of Uššur-ana-Marduk, blessed by god and king, the humble, the obedient, the one who pleases his lord, took up residence in a distinguished manner in the house which I had erected in the shadow of the temple of Marduk, within which I had opened a well of cold water, which I had staked off by the exalted wisdom of the god Marduk, my lord. I had made the burnt brick rooms beneath it, about which no one knows, with wise understanding and the greatest care. I constructed and completed the entire house, its reception suites and residential quarters. I will not allow imbeciles to take possession (of it).

Does the last sentence betray chauvinism of this Babylonian luminary against his Assyrian neighbours?

Royal hostages and an accidental tourist in Aššur, 1112 BC

In the first example of a new type of inscription that structured the narrative in chronological order (hence 'Assyrian Annals') and gave a summary of the king's deeds for each year of his reign up until the time that the text was composed, Tiglath-pileser I details how he led an expeditionary force deep into Anatolia in 1112 BC. On the plain of Manzikert to the north of Lake Van, best known as the battlefield where the Seljuq Sultan Alp Arslan annihilated the Byzantine army in AD 1071, the Assyrian king, too, celebrated a triumph. He defeated an alliance of twenty-three local rulers there. His account of the battle ends with this passage:

> I captured all the kings of Nairi (= Anatolia) alive. I had mercy on them and spared their lives. I released them from their bonds and

> fetters before the sun god, my lord, and made them swear an oath
> of everlasting servitude by my great gods. I took their royal sons as
> hostages. I imposed on them a tribute of 1,200 horses and 2,000
> cattle. I allowed them to return to their lands.

The defeated rulers had to accept Assyrian sovereignty and concluded a treaty with their new overlord. An oath and their children's placement as hostages protected the agreement which stipulated the regular delivery of cattle and horses, urgently needed in Assyria for the chariotry and, in later times from the 9th century onwards, for the cavalry (see Chapter 6). The Anatolian hostages were to be raised at the royal court of Assyria where their presence served a twofold purpose. While in Assyria, they were to guarantee their families', and countries', loyalty with their lives. And when they returned to their native land, ideally as its ruler or in another influential position, the time spent at the Assyrian court would have attuned them to Assyrian sensibilities and thus ensured their dependable conduct at home.

This is especially well attested in the early 7th century BC when several former hostages returned to rule their native country in line with Assyria's wishes: Bel-ibni, whom Sennacherib appointed as king of Babylon in 703 BC, 'had grown up like a puppy in my palace' (or, given the timing, rather his father Sargon's palace), while Tabua, whom Esarhaddon made queen of the Arabs, 'was raised in the palace of my father (Sennacherib)' according to the royal inscriptions. These royal hostages had been children when they were sent to the Assyrian court—an obvious advantage for the objective of pro-Assyrian indoctrination. But the distinction between hostage and protégé could be somewhat blurred. On occasion, foreign dynasts saw the Assyrian court as a safe haven for their children, especially in times of upheaval back home. Balassu, leader of the southern Babylonian tribe of Bit-Dakkuri, for example, sent his son and daughter to Sargon II for their protection when his enemy Merodach-baladan, of the rival Bit-Yakin tribe, proclaimed himself king of Babylon.

Tiglath-pileser I's inscription about the Anatolian campaign continued:

> I brought Seni, king of Daienu, who had not been submissive to the god Aššur, my lord, in bonds and fetters to my city Aššur. I had mercy on him and let him leave my city Aššur alive in order to proclaim the glory of the great gods.

One of the Anatolian kings, it would seem, needed to be taught a special lesson. Unlike his twenty-two allies, he was brought to Aššur. Does the reference to his not being submissive mean that he refused to swear the loyalty oath and was he therefore taken as a punishment? Or would this classification have equally applied to all the other Anatolian rulers and the visit to the Assyrian capital was a special distinction? However that may be, after Seni's sojourn to Aššur he was sent back home. There, he was to sing the praise of the gods and presumably of Assyria and its king, of whose power a visit to the capital would have given Seni a fair idea.

Such visits to central Assyria were a typical experience for rulers who had been made to accept Assyrian sovereignty. The imagery of the royal palaces from Aššurnasirpal II onwards was specifically designed to make an impact on them. Chaotic scenes of conquest and surrender on the one hand and orderly scenes of royal audiences and delivery of tribute on the other showed the two modes of interaction with Assyrian power, and it was the latter that was meant to appeal to the foreign visitors.

An Iranian family in Aššur, 715–614 BC

We have already encountered in Chapter 3 members of the substantial Egyptian community living in Aššur, relocated there after the Assyrian conquest of Memphis in 671 BC. They were not the first foreigners from beyond the Semitic-speaking world of Mesopotamia and Syro-Palestina to be settled in the ancient city.

Already, forty years earlier, in the aftermath of the creation of two Assyrian provinces in the region of modern Hamadan in western Iran, people from these Median territories had been brought 500 kilometres westwards, across the Zagros mountains to Aššur in 715 BC.

The initial situation in the provinces of Harhar and Kišessim, which Sargon II had established in 716, was dangerously volatile, as the king's correspondence with his governors and vassals in the area illustrates. The Assyrian administration struggled with the harsh weather that slowed down the establishment of the necessary infrastructure, and snow in the Zagros cut the new provinces off from the Assyrian heartland for parts of the year. Already in 715 the new provinces rose in rebellion against the fledgling Assyrian government and the imperial army returned. The intervention was very bloody and, according to the inscriptions of Sargon II, 4,000 enemy warriors were beheaded. A further 4,820 persons were selected for relocation (see Chapter 6), and this brought some of them to the city of Aššur.

One extended family from Hundir, the hinterland of Kišessim, moved into houses within the monumental gateway leading into the north-western part of Aššur—erected in this somewhat awkward location because it had become increasingly difficult to find suitable accommodation elsewhere in the cramped city. Walter Andrae excavated these buildings in 1906 while investigating the city's fortifications. He found them well preserved, as the city wall, against which they leaned, had collapsed at some point after 614 BC and buried them. The houses and especially the documents found there give us insight into the Iranian clan living there. In the 620s the household consisted of the members of three generations and their twenty-one slaves, a total of at least thirty-five permanent residents. The family is known in detail because of two legal documents recording the division of the estate left by family head Mudammiq-Aššur to his six sons. This was a well-to-do family spread out over two sizeable houses. With the ground floors taking up areas of 240 m^2 and 320 m^2 respectively, they lived in considerably grander style than their contemporary, the wine merchant Duri-Aššur (see Chapter 3).

Since the arrival of the Medes at Aššur, the men of the family held positions at the Aššur temple (as did most of the city's notables), but as their professional title was 'Hundurean', after their place of origin, it is not clear what their actual occupation was. They worked with a certain type of textile that may have been a kind of rug. If this is correct then perhaps they introduced to central Assyria the art of hand-knotting carpets with a pile. The family was also involved in overland trade but unlike in the case of Duri-Aššur's wine firm, the destination of their caravans is not mentioned in the records. As caravan staff were given working contracts of seven–twelve months, which covered both legs of the trip, these were long-distance journeys. Given the family's origins, it seems most likely that they were trading with their Iranian homeland. After all, the Median centres Harhar and Kišessim had been renamed by their conqueror Sargon II: Kar-Šarrukin, 'Sargon's Harbour,' and Kar-Nergal, 'Harbour of the God Nergal' (using the conventional designation for trading posts; see Chapter 2) in appreciation of their role in the overland trade along an important stage of the Silk Route.

The distinct cultural heritage of the Egyptians, including names, deities, and material culture was still apparent decades after their arrival; but the Iranian clan, who of course had arrived at Aššur two generations before the Egyptian community, used—at least by the second half of the 7th century—only Assyrian names invoking Assyrian deities, and no recognizably Iranian material was found in the remains of their houses. Although such evidence would seem to suggest that the family embraced the Assyrian lifestyle, it is also clear that the Medes at Aššur preserved some part of their Iranian identity: they maintained their own distinct occupation (whatever its nature) and also traded with the old country.

The sources tell us nothing about their role in the Median assault on Aššur or their fate after the conquest in 614. It is tempting to link the swift success of the siege with the fact that Medes lived inside one of the city's principal gates and were therefore in a prime position to help the besiegers enter the city. After all, it is otherwise surprising that the Medes succeeded so swiftly when the Babylonian army had failed to take Aššur during its surprise attack in the previous year, especially as the city's fortifications and food reserves had been increased in anticipation of a further attack.

Two female prisoners of war, sold as slaves, c.645 BC

By now, we have encountered a great many slaves who were ubiquitous throughout the cities of the Assyrian Empire. In Assyrian society, owning slaves was an indication of wealth and social status, and slave owners were generally members of the urban elite. In this section, we will focus on two of them, mother and daughter, and trace their how they came to live in Aššur as slaves. Like many Assyrian slaves, they were of foreign extraction. But native free-born Assyrians, too, could be sold into slavery as a last resort in lieu of debt; they could be released if they, or someone else on their behalf, paid up. Most slaves that we encounter in the sources served as domestic staff and lived in their owner's house. A slave woman's child was born a slave, regardless of who the father was. Often, this will have been the owner. He could adopt the child if he wanted to acknowledge his offspring, and only in that case would the child have had the right to inherit. This happened rarely, usually if there were no legitimate sons, and the wife's consent was needed, as stipulations in marriage contracts indicate.

Between 664 and 648 BC, Assyrian forces repeatedly invaded and plundered the south-western Iranian kingdom of Elam. After a brief period of peace under Esarhaddon the two states were in a state of war during much of Aššurbanipal's early reign, documented in royal inscriptions, on the wall decorations of his palaces in Nineveh, and in letters of the state correspondence. A private legal text from Aššur documents the fate of one woman and her daughter who were caught up in the wars and taken away from Elam as captives. In the document recording their sale (for one mina (*c.*500 grams) of silver, an average price in the mid-7th century), they are described as 'booty from Elam whom the king had given to Libbali (i.e. the city of Aššur)'. Depictions on the palace wall decoration frequently show how after battle, administrators registered and distributed the spoils, including human captives. But the further fortunes of individual prisoners of war are hard to trace in the sources, and the case of the two Elamite captives is a rare example that highlights the effects of war on women.

The sale contract's date is lost but its context suggests that Nanaya-ila'i and her child were snatched during the sack of Susa in 646 BC when enormous amounts of booty were captured. When they reached Aššur as part of the booty contingent reserved for that city, our text documents that ten men owned them jointly and sold them to one man, Mannu-ki-Aššur. The sellers, identified by name and profession, were a group of various temple craftsmen, among them a baker, a cook, a weaver, a goldsmith, an ironsmith, and a shepherd. Although they were of course all serving the Aššur temple, they had otherwise little in common. However, as there are ten of them and because a military connection links them to the Elamite captives, we may assume that they constituted a work unit (*kiṣru*, literally 'knot') that fulfilled their work obligations to the state, including military service, as a group. As part of the contingent from Aššur, they may have participated in a military campaign against Elam (most likely as non-combatant maintenance staff; see Chapter 6) and received the Elamite captives as their reward from the battle spoils reserved for their city. As owning the slaves jointly was of limited practical use to the men, selling them and dividing the proceeds was the obvious solution and the sale took place as soon as the Elamite captives arrived at Aššur.

From then on, Nanaya-ila'i and her daughter spent their lives as domestic slaves in Mannu-ki-Aššur's household. Their fate was very different from, say, the Medes or Egyptians who had been settled in Aššur. The latter may have had little say in their relocation but once there, they were 'counted among the Assyrians' and had the same rights and duties as the other free inhabitants. They were not slaves, in contrast to war spoils like Nanaya-ila'i and her daughter. The woman's name means 'The goddess Nanaya is my deity'. It was certainly not her original one and Nanaya-ila'i will only have received it once she had come into Assyrian captivity. The name is a deliberate reference to Aššurbanipal's widely publicized repatriation of an ancient statue of the goddess Nanaya that had been abducted over a millennium ago to Elam. Her daughter's name was not given, which suggests that she was quite young and considered dependent on her mother. She was likely older than four years as she is neither identified as a baby ('Of the milk' or 'Of the breast') nor as a toddler ('Separated', referring to being weaned from the breast).

Just as Nanaya-ila'i was stripped of her name, she will have lost much that constituted her previous identity. We know nothing about her original social background in Elam. But at least she was not separated from her child. This was usual practice in Assyrian slave sales, certainly as long as the children were small. In this specific case it was sensible to keep mother and daughter together because it would have made integrating the foreigners easier into their new environment. Elamite is a language entirely unrelated to Semitic languages like Assyrian and Aramaic that were widely spoken in Aššur. This makes it unlikely that Nanaya-ila'i would have been able to communicate fluently in her new surroundings. Given her young age, her daughter would have picked up the local languages more easily and facilitated also her mother's integration.

In their new life, the two Elamites contributed to the everyday running of the household of their master Mannu-ki-Aššur.

Nothing else is known about this man but given that he was from Aššur, he probably lived in a house rather like the ones owned by the wine merchant Duri-Aššur (see Chapter 3) or the Median family already discussed. His family will have had a number of slaves but the Elamites were certainly not part of a household numbering scores of people, unlike the one inhabiting Šulmu-šarri's gigantic mansion in Dur-Katlimmu (see Chapter 3). Nanaya-ila'i and her daughter would have spent their time performing household chores: grinding flour, baking, cooking, and sweeping, and they may have added to the household's prosperity by spinning wool and weaving textiles that could be sold at a profit. We may imagine their existence as a quiet one, a relief after the trauma of their wartime experiences and their abduction to the Assyrian heartland. But unless she died early (for example during childbirth, as happened frequently), Nanaya-ila'i's daughter would have witnessed another invasion, the conquest of Aššur in 614 BC. She may well have been claimed as booty again, this time by the Median army who would have taken her back east into Iran.

Chapter 6
Assyrian world domination: pathfinder empire

The Assyrian Empire, as it was configured in the 9th century BC, was the pathfinder among the sequence of empires subsequently dominating the wider Mediterranean and Middle East, including the Persian and the Roman empires. Its ideological, infrastructural, and organizational innovations provided the basis and template for the successor states. Winning an empire is a challenge, but making it cohere is an even bigger one, and Assyria faced this task with aplomb. This final chapter is devoted to key aspects of governance and ideology that contributed to the fact that the Assyrian Empire managed to control its holdings for three centuries. Warfare is prominently reviewed in sources such as Assyrian palace art, royal inscriptions, and the Bible, and we will have a closer look at the empire's fabled army. The ideology of absolute kingship, the innovative long-distance relay postal service and the empire-wide resettlement programme provided powerful tools for the empire's cohesion. The final section deals with the royal library that the Assyrian kings assembled and maintained from the 14th century BC. Since its rediscovery in the mid-19th century by the indefatigable Henry Austen Layard, it has contributed much to our knowledge of Assyria's cultural history. If a love of books played any role at all in the library's creation then it was certainly not the only motivation.

The 'hosts of Aššur'—an ancient army you'd rather not join?

When Assyria emerged as a territorial power in the 14th century BC, the bulk of its armed forces consisted of an infantry mustered from conscripted farmers and of a chariotry led by members of the leading families who fought with bow and arrow. The second member of the chariot crew, the driver, was apparently a dependant of the fighter. He was always mentioned in second place and, unlike the fighters who were so well known that they often needed no further qualification in archival documents, usually identified by military title. The chariotry of that age can be seen as semi-professional in that its members had to spend a good deal of time exercising their skill. But it remains unclear whether they were permanently stationed or, as seems more likely, only assembled when called up by the king. The conscripts drafted from the tax-paying population could provide military service only during the summer months when the agricultural calendar permitted the absence of farm workers. They were organized into units based on the decimal system (10, 50, 100), and the resultant social structures counterbalanced the importance of the family and were a forceful reminder of the impact of the state on each individual's life. The entire armed forces were structured in this way.

The mid-9th century BC saw the definitive shift from an army dominated by temporarily mobilized conscripts to one largely consisting of fighters maintained all year round. Shalmaneser III established standing armies that were permanently stationed in vulnerable border regions. In doing so, he also drew on captured specialized fighters who had been absorbed into the Assyrian army during a century of conquest. At the same time, the first Assyrian cavalry units were created. The integration of fighters from defeated regions into the permanent forces continued routinely and focused on chariotry and mounted troops, that is those fighters with the most specialized training. Once the expansion begun under Tiglath-pileser III had resulted in doubling Assyria's former holdings, the standing armed forces were so numerous that the tax-paying population was no longer required for temporary military service and mostly used for civilian purposes, such as public building works. No longer dependent on personnel tied to the agricultural calendar, campaigning was now possible also outside of the summer months, enabling much longer military operations to much further destinations, such as Egypt.

The Assyrian army of the first millennium BC was really many armies, termed poetically the 'Hosts of the God Aššur' in the royal inscriptions. The different contingents were allowed to preserve and develop their own customs and idiosyncrasies. Rather than being forged into a unified army, its individual components found themselves in intense competition with each other for royal recognition and favour. This strategy aimed at neutralizing the armed forces' otherwise unbridled power vis-à-vis king and state: a useful and successful policy that significantly contributed to Assyria's internal stability and the longevity of its royal dynasty. The different bodies of the army were structured into smaller contingents led by officers, at least some of whom were promoted from the ordinary ranks. The basic command unit numbered fifty men. One can distinguish between the 'Royal Cohort' that the king himself commanded and the armies he placed under the authority of others. Although troops were stationed at forts set up in strategic border locations, the provinces were not permanently garrisoned and the provincial governors controlled troops only in the short term, either mobilized temporarily or brought in from elsewhere. An efficient defensive system concentrated the bulk of the standing army in four strategically located border marches established during the reign of Shalmaneser III.

Alongside the Assyrian contingents fought auxiliaries from adjoining regions and internal peripheries (steppes, deserts, mountains). These were of great importance and in the main assumed the role of the infantry that conscripted fighters had held previously. The empire cultivated long-standing relationships with certain auxiliary units. But the politics of the day and opportunity certainly influenced the use of auxiliaries as well. Hence, the forces mustered by Sennacherib during his war in Judah in 701 BC, as depicted in the siege of Lachish on the walls of his Southwest Palace in Nineveh, included auxiliary contingents of slingers, specialized infantry fighters using slingshots that were typical of that very region, as the Biblical story of David's victory over Goliath best illustrates. In the palace wall decorations, auxiliary troops can be easily distinguished from Assyrian troops by their dress. While the latter wear standardized uniforms together with the typical conical helmet, the auxiliaries are always shown wearing their own specific clothes. In Assyrian art, warfare is a matter for grown-ups: all warriors are shown as mature men in their physical prime, with full beards (unless they are eunuchs; see Chapter 2), and heavily muscled.

In terms of specialization, the imperial army consisted of the chariotry, the cavalry, and the infantry divided into ranged archers and close combat spearmen. The term for spearmen was 'Bearer of shield and spear', referencing the typical armoured shield and spear, but this was often abbreviated to 'Shield-bearer'. These fighters closely correspond to the Greek hoplites. The term for chariotry is simply the designation for chariot while the cavalry is called after the riding horse (literally, 'The one opening one's thighs'). All of these troops were professional fighters. Various textual sources suggest that a ratio of 1:10:200 for chariotry, cavalry, and infantry, with the latter divided 2:1 into archers and spearmen, was considered an ideal balance. However, the armed forces were mustered to suit specific objectives and an appropriate selection of troops was dispatched accordingly. When on the move, the Assyrian army lived in tents inside fortified camps that were temporarily constructed. Building the camp was one of the tasks of the non-combatant support staff, some recruited from conscripts, that constituted a very large part of the armed forces.

Every provincial capital maintained food and fodder storage facilities for the use of the army. Abroad, the troops and their animals lived off the land by foraging as bulky supplies were kept to a minimum while travelling.

Chariots manned by archers continued to be used in the Assyrian armed forces from the late second to the first millennium BC, without disruption and little change in equipment and tactical use. In the plains of Mesopotamia and Syria the chariot's twin advantages of speed and manoeuvrability continued to make it an excellent weapon of attack. The cavalry, on the other hand, was established as a regular component of the army only in the 9th century under Shalmaneser III. The light and brittle construction of a chariot and its lack of suspension made driving this expensive vehicle in mountainous landscapes impossible as the resultant damage to the wheels would immobilize it completely. Chariots had to be disassembled in order to be transported in such terrain, rendering them inconvenient ballast rather than dangerous weapons. The cavalry grew out of the attempt to develop a rough terrain chariot suitable for the rugged landscapes of the Taurus and Zagros regions—key arenas of conflict since the emergence of Urartu, Mannea, and the Medes in the 9th century BC. The earliest depictions of Assyrian cavalry on Shalmaneser III's bronze decoration of the temple gates at Balawat near Kalhu, show teams of two riders operating like a chariot would (one serving the role of the 'driver', one as the archer), but without the terrain limitations of the chariot's physical body.

The chariot troops retained their value in the plains, but by the mid-8th century the more economical and more mobile cavalry had replaced the light chariotry in the battlefield. Chariots were now armoured and manned by teams of three: the chariot driver, the fighter, and the so-called 'Third Man' who shielded the others. In the 7th century BC chariots were still maintained in the hundreds but now even more heavily armoured, drawn by four horses and with a fourth man on the chariot team providing additional protection. These tank-like constructions were much taller than previous models, with wheel diameters of close to two metres, and were used to shoot at enemy archers at close range, serving, moreover, very effectively the twin purposes of show-of-force and intimidation.

Chariot troops, cavalry, and the majority of the infantry fought with bow and arrow, using a traditional composite model with a triangular profile and a length of 110–125 cm. The bow was therefore the most important weapon of the Assyrian forces, and this fact should inform all considerations of their tactics in pitched battle. However, the biased nature of the sources makes any attempt to reconstruct particular battles inherently problematic.

Sea warfare played a relatively minor role. The first Assyrian fleet was constructed in 694 and deployed in the Persian Gulf. Ships built by Syrian craftsmen at Nineveh and manned with crews of Phoenicians and 'Ionians' (probably a general term for Greeks) were sailed down the Tigris to Babylonia, then transported overland to a side arm of the Euphrates and from there sailed to the Persian Gulf to mount a surprise attack on the coast of Elam in Iran. The ships were presumably biremes (galleys with two decks of oars), as routinely depicted on the palace wall decoration. In the Mediterranean, the empire relied on collaboration with its Phoenician clients, especially Tyre. Assyria did not maintain a Mediterranean navy of its own until Sidon was annexed in 677 and established as an Assyrian port, under the new name 'Esarhaddon's Harbour'. The hold over Sidon was used to provide rearguard for the land-led invasion of Egypt.

Siege warfare, on the other hand, was a key tactic of the Assyrian forces but even more so the threat of siege. Without catapults (widely used only from the early 4th century BC onwards) or any other kind of heavy artillery that could be deployed from a safe distance, the only option was to overcome or destroy the fortifications while operating within reach of the defenders.

11. Capture of a fortified Egyptian city on the Nile and its aftermath, the arrest of Nubian soldiers from Kush and the deportation of the civilian Egyptian population. From King Aššurbanipal's North Palace in Nineveh.

Depictions of sieges on the palace wall decorations (Figure 11) show an impressive arsenal of battering rams and manned siege engines, ladders, and mobile siege towers as well as sapping and tunnelling. These images were designed to create the impression that Assyrian conquest was inevitable. The popular view of the Assyrian Empire rarely goes beyond the impression gained from these images, resulting—absolutely in line with the intent of their creators—in the perception of a people hell-bent on conquest. This is, for example, the key message of *You Wouldn't Want to Be an Assyrian Soldier: An Ancient Army You'd Rather Not Join*, by Rupert Matthews and David Antram, a rare, and amusing, example of a children's book dealing with Assyria.

However, if a fortified city had to be taken entirely by force, without help from within, the cost would have been very high. Consequently, sieges were avoided whenever possible, as for example oracle queries (see Chapter 3) indicate. Various methods were used to persuade the besieged to surrender. Promises of amnesty were honoured if accepted; resettling the population was not considered punishment. If this did not yield results, the trees in the fruit orchards and palm tree plantations outside the city walls were put to the axe one by one. As these take many years to yield fruit, this lastingly damaged the livelihood of the besieged community. Finally, selected prisoners of war or hostages were executed in plain sight of the defenders. The method of choice was live impalement, but it is clear that most sieges ended before it came to this. If the besieged did not yield, as for example the cities of Babylon and Nippur over several years during the war between Aššurbanipal and his brother Šamaš-šumu-ukin for control over Babylonia, then famine and disease quickly made life in the enclosed cities harrowing and unremittingly bleak.

The blessed king: absolute monarchy

When Aššurnasirpal II relocated the court from Aššur to Kalhu in 879 BC, the images decorating the throne room of his new palace were consciously designed to promote a crucial twofold ideological message. Firstly, that Aššurnasirpal II controlled all lands. We have already highlighted the opposition between the orderly, calm scenes of audiences and tribute delivery that show the king interacting with his dutiful clients and the chaotic, violent scenes of conquest and siege that illustrate how the king reacted to resistance. Secondly, the throne room was to emphasize that despite the move away from the temple of Aššur, the relationship between the god and the king, his chosen representative, was as close and strong as ever.

To this end, a remarkable scene was depicted twice in the throne room (Figure 12), once on the wall opposite the entrance along the longer side of the oblong hall and again at its far end, above the platform on which the royal throne rested. As visitors entered the room, their glance was therefore directed forcefully onto the heraldic, mirrored image that showed Aššurnasirpal (twice) with the god Aššur. The king, guarded by a winged protective spirit,

12. The king in communion with the god Aššur. From King Aššurnasirpal II's throne room in the Northwest Palace at Kalhu.

raises his right hand in the typical gesture of worship to the deity; this scene is shown twice on either side of the god. Aššur is shown in human yet disembodied form as the divine counterpart to the king in the guise of a bearded man wearing the distinctive fez-like headdress of the Assyrian ruler and holding the king's weapons of choice, the bow and arrow. A winged disc surrounds the figure, emphasizing the deity's ethereal otherworldliness, and hovers above an enigmatic emblem that is today called Sacred Tree or Tree of Life (although it does not really look like a tree at all). This imagery powerfully suggests that the king did not need the temple of Aššur in order to commune with the god. So strong was their link that the blessed king himself served as a conduit. With Aššur's blessing, his power was absolute.

But it did not need an audience with the king in Kalhu to come across this potent image. A carnelian cylinder seal (Figure 13) of the local ruler of Šadikanni (from Tell Ajaja on the Khabur in north-eastern Syria) demonstrates that the image was disseminated across the empire in the form of easily portable art. The seal bears the inscription in cuneiform script of Mušezib-Ninurta, son of Ninurta-ereš, grandson of Samanuha-šar-ilani, members of an

13. Carnelian cylinder seal with a cuneiform inscription, showing a scene modelled on that from the throne room of Aššurnasirpal II.

ancient dynasty that ruled over the city of Šadikanni. Samanuha-šar-ilani was a contemporary of Aššurnasirpal, attested as an Assyrian ally in the reconquest of the Khabur region in the account for the year 883 in the Assyrian king's inscriptions. His grandson was presumably a contemporary of Aššurnasirpal's long-lived successor Shalmaneser III. The inscription was engraved in the positive on the seal, meaning that it was impressed in mirror writing when the seal was used. This suggests that the text was not an original part of the seal design and it may have been added at a considerably later time. A likely scenario is that Aššurnasirpal bestowed the precious object as a gift on his ally, for the seal shows a scene modelled on the heraldic design displayed in the throne room of Aššurnasirpal's palace at Kalhu.

By (at least) the 7th century, royal ideology saw the king as a being quite separate from ordinary humans and superior to them. In a literary text about the creation of man, the gods fashioned the king in a separate act after having already created mankind:

Ea (god of wisdom) opened his mouth to speak, saying a word to Belet-ili (goddess of creation): 'You are Belet-ili, the sister of the great gods; it was you who created man, the human (*lullû amēlu*). Fashion now the king, the counsellor man (*šarru māliku amēlu*)! Gird the whole of his figure so pleasingly, make perfect his countenance and well formed his body!' And Belet-ili fashioned the king, the counsellor man.

The blessed royal family held a very special status in Assyrian society and only its male members were eligible for kingship. Although there were usurpations and succession wars, all Assyrian kings until the end of the empire are descended from this one family through the male line, making it one of the longest serving royal houses of all time.

Long-distance express communication

A key strategy for ensuring cohesion across the vast Assyrian Empire was fast communication connecting the king with the governors in the provinces and the ambassadors at the client rulers' courts abroad. The imperial communication network was carefully planned and created in the 9th century BC and known as the 'King's Road'. The governors had to maintain road stations in strategic positions within their province that served as stages and intersections in the imperial communication system; whenever a new province was added to the realm, it was one of the key challenges of the new administration to connect it to the 'King's Road'. The road stations were either situated within existing settlements or constituted settlements of their own, with the necessary agricultural basis to provide for personnel, envoys, and transport animals. The caravanserais of the medieval Muslim world may serve as a convenient comparison, in that they, too, are purpose-built structures along long-distance routes providing short-term shelter and protection for travellers and their animals, but a crucial difference is that the Assyrian road stations served only the state and were not open to commercial travellers.

The circle of people allowed to make use of the resources of the 'King's Road' was therefore restricted and only available to those who had been formally appointed to a state office. The magnates of the empire all received a copy of a signet ring engraved with the universally recognized imperial emblem (showing the king killing a lion; see Figure 10) as a symbol of their office and as a tool to act in the king's stead. They used this ring to seal their letters, and this enabled all those playing a role in the transmission of their missives, such as the personnel of the road stations and the king's secretaries, to instantly identify them as a letters of state importance, treating them with the required attention and urgency.

Messages were exchanged either by letter only, passed on from courier to courier, or by envoy (who might or might not carry a letter). Sending an envoy, who travelled the whole distance, was the preferred means of communication when the message was very sensitive or when it was important that a decision could be made on the spot. The king's 'Friends' (see Chapter 3) often served as his envoys. The first method was considerably faster, as each courier travelled only one stage of the distance from one past station to the next, where the letter was passed on to a new courier, enabling the message to travel without delay. The disassociation between letter and messenger was an Assyrian innovation of the 9th century BC, radical at the time. Until the advent of the telegraph, this relay system set the standard for communication speed for almost three millennia.

The couriers and envoys were mounted, travelling with pairs of mules in order to reduce the possibility that the rider was ever left stranded with a lame animal. The offspring of a horse mother and a donkey father, these infertile hybrids combine the body of a horse with the extremities of a donkey and often grow taller than the parents. Mules mature five years later than the parent animals but have a longer working life of up to twenty years. Infertile, slow to develop physically and in need of extensive yet sensitive training, mules were an expensive investment. For the Assyrian state, however, the expense was easily offset by the fact that mules are stronger and more resilient than horses, while sharing the donkey's sure-footedness and instinct for self-preservation; they are also good swimmers. The military use of these animals has continued into the present, for example, in the British and the US armies.

The king's correspondents used the expensive communication system only when they needed to involve the central administration in their decision-making or in order to pass on essential information. The magnates were appointed in order to exercise power locally on behalf of the crown and, in doing so, were meant to rely on their own judgement. Their main duty was to act on behalf of the king wherever and whenever he himself could not be present. Most of their letters therefore deal with the unexpected rather than with routine matters: opportunities arising and catastrophes unfolding, turns of events that galvanize or, on occasion, stupefy the wardens of the Assyrian Empire. Many of the letters therefore focus on problems, hiccups, and challenges.

About 2,000 letters from the state correspondence of the first millennium are presently known. These letters are rather unevenly distributed over two centuries, from the reign of Adad-nerari III in the early 8th century to the end of the empire. Most of the state letters, about 1,200 texts, date to the reign of Sargon II. Most of these were found as part of the royal archives at Nineveh, where they had been moved to under Sargon's successor Sennacherib, but a smaller part of his correspondence has been excavated at Kalhu. These texts are one of the best sources available for historians studying how an ancient empire was run.

Counting them as Assyrians: the resettlement programme

All people of the empire, no matter their origin, were 'counted among the Assyrians', as the royal inscriptions put it. The Bible quotes a message that King Sennacherib supposedly communicated to the people of Jerusalem during the siege of 701 BC. After urging them to abandon his treacherous vassal, their king Hezekiah of Judah, he said:

> Make peace with me and come out to me. Then each of you will eat fruit from your own vine and fig tree and drink water from your own cistern, until I come and take you to a land like your own—a land of grain and new wine, a land of bread and vineyards, a land of olive trees and honey. Choose life and not death! (2 Kings 18: 31–2)

'Deportation', as the strategy of mass resettlement in the Assyrian Empire is usually called (a misnomer, given various inapplicable associations such as marginalization and extermination), could indeed be regarded as a privilege rather than a punishment. People moved together with their families and their possessions (see Figure 11); they were not snatched away in the heat of battle or conquest, but were chosen as the result of a deliberate selection process, often in the aftermath of a war that had very possibly reduced their original home to ruins; and when the Assyrian sources specify who was to be relocated, they name the urban elites, craftsmen, scholars, and military men. The resettlement policy divided communities into those who had to stay and those who had to leave, according to the needs of the empire. The specialists from newly subjugated areas were most frequently resettled in the Assyrian heartland to the economic and cultural benefit of the empire, to generate knowledge and wealth.

On the other hand, disgraced Assyrians, rather than being killed, were sent away from their home in order to redeem themselves as colonists in the state's service. In complex circular movements that were carefully planned and executed over several years, populations were relocated within the boundaries of the empire, replacing and being replaced by people who were themselves moved. For example, inhabitants of Samaria, conquered in 722 BC, were moved to the two provinces Harhar and Kiššesim created in Median territory in the Hamadan region in Iran in 716 BC. People from there were in turn settled in Aššur (see Chapter 5), from whence some people, pardoned after a failed insurrection in 720 BC, had been relocated to Hamath (modern Hama in Syria) which had rebelled at the same time and been destroyed as a result. Its inhabitants were moved to Samaria, closing this circuit. It is only one strand of vastly complex, simultaneous arrangements that included also regions in Babylonia and Anatolia. It has been calculated on the basis of references in the royal inscriptions that 4,400,000 ± 900,000 people were relocated from the mid-9th to the mid-7th century BC, of which 85 per cent were settled in central Assyria—a gigantic number, especially in a world whose population was a small fraction of today's. For all of these people, resettlement was meant to provide a better future while at the same time benefitting the empire. Of course, their relocation was at the same time an effective way of minimizing the risk of rebellion against the central authority.

The settlers, their labour, and their abilities were extremely valuable to the state. Their relocation was carefully planned and organized. They were to travel comfortably and safely in order to reach their destination in good physical shape. In the depictions decorating the palace walls, men, women, and children are shown travelling in groups, often riding on vehicles or animals, and never in bonds. The travel provisions for one group of settlers from western Syria were the subject of an 8th century letter from an official to King Tiglath-pileser III:

> As for the Arameans about whom the king my lord has written to me: 'Prepare them for their journey!' I shall give them their food

supplies, clothes, a waterskin, a pair of shoes and oil. I do not have my donkeys yet, but once they are available, I will dispatch my convoy.

That the state also supported the settlers once they had reached their destination is clear from another letter of the same correspondence:

As for the Arameans about whom the king my lord has said: 'They are to have wives!' We found numerous suitable women but their fathers refuse to give them in marriage, claiming: 'We will not consent unless they can pay the bride price.' Let them be paid so that the Arameans can get married.

This statement highlights how the state actively encouraged a mixing of the new neighbours. The ultimate goal of the Assyrian resettlement policy was to create a homogeneous population of 'Assyrians' with a shared culture and a common identity.

Knowledge and power: the royal library

If the discovery of the palace sculpture made Assyria popular and resulted in best-selling books and crowded exhibitions in the mid-19th century AD, the recovery of the extensive archives and libraries from the royal palaces of Nineveh and their decipherment heralded the foundation of a new academic discipline dubbed Assyriology. While its core had been gradually assembled over centuries, the collection is today called the 'Library of Aššurbanipal', after the most avid among the royal collectors. The once substantial holdings of wax-boards (see Chapter 2) have been completely lost to the fires engulfing the palaces on Nineveh in 612 and the ravages of time. But about 20,000 library tablets have survived and are today kept in the British Museum as part of its 'Kuyunjik Collection' (named after the settlement mound housing the palaces of Nineveh). Although much has been published, the library is so vast that it is still impossible to give a fully informed overview of its contents. It is, however, certain that only a tiny minority of texts can be called literature, including the famous Epic of Gilgameš, whereas ritual instructions and the prognostic disciplines of astrology and sacrificial divination emerge as the key subject areas from the published part of the library. The collection's primary function was to provide the scholarly advisers of the king with materials to support royal decision-making and secure divine favour for king and state: texts containing detailed guidelines for the performance of rituals or huge reference collections of omens.

All Assyrian kings, at least in the 8th and 7th centuries BC, were cuneiform literate, as were the other men destined for a role in the running of the empire. However, Aššurbanipal's fascination with esoteric and arcane knowledge went far beyond basic literacy. In his inscriptions, he claimed to have undergone an extensive scholarly education. Moreover, in some of the wall decorations of his North Palace in Nineveh, he had himself depicted with a writing stylus tucked into his belt, instead of the more usual knife. But the beginnings of the Assyrian royal library likely reached back to the 14th century BC and King Aššur-uballit I, whose Royal Scribe Marduk-nadin-ahhe from Babylon (see Chapter 5) would have been well placed to initiate such a project. When Tukulti-Ninurta I sacked Babylon in the 13th century BC, he brought back library tablets to add to the holdings, and by the 7th century, the collection had grown into the biggest cuneiform library of all times.

For the most part, the royal library was the product of local Assyrian copying, editing, and composing. But Aššurbanipal also made focused use of the empire's control over Babylonia, and perhaps Egypt, to collect library texts. So organized was this effort that the king had search parties dispatched in order to locate rare scholarly works and appropriate them, by force if needed. Records listing 2,000 tablets and 300 writing-boards demonstrate that these were integrated into the royal library after the end of the

Babylonian insurrection from 652 to 648 BC (see Chapter 4) from private collections. In addition, Babylonians were drafted into the existing large-scale programme of copying tablets. Some were commissioned and paid to produce tablets, but others were forced to do so. One administrative text reveals that captive Babylonians 'in fetters' were made to copy tablets under duress, including the son of the governor of Nippur who had supported the rebellion. This sheds some light on the treatment of political prisoners at Nineveh and also illustrates that the members of the urban Babylonian elite were highly educated. Well-read gentleman scholar Aššurbanipal was certainly not a unique case.

By the beginning of the 7th century BC, the central Assyrian cities of Nineveh, Kalhu, and Aššur housed experts from all over the known world. Without them, some of the most enduring achievements of the Assyrian kings, such as constructing and furnishing the magnificent palaces and temples or assembling the contents of the fabled library of Aššurbanipal, would have been impossible. Regardless of whether he was motivated by a thirst for knowledge and the wish to control and utilize this knowledge in the interest of the empire, or whether he indulged in the wealthy collector's voraciousness, today the library is Aššurbanipal's and perhaps Assyria's most lasting monument.

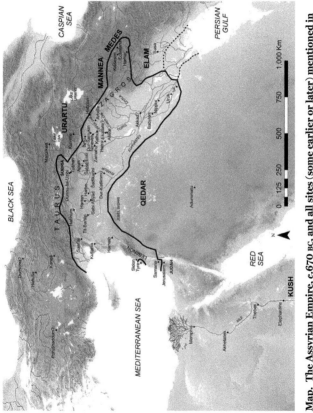

Map. The Assyrian Empire, *c*.670 BC, and all sites (some earlier or later) mentioned in this volume.

Timeline

Rulers of Aššur

...

Ušpia late 3rd millennium BC	Builds Aššur temple	
...		
Erišum I 19th century	Enlarges Aššur temple	Merchants in Kaneš: level Ib
...		
Samsi-Addu 18th century	Conquers Aššur; rebuilds temple	Merchants in Kaneš: level II
Išme-Dagan 18th century		Hammurabi, king of Babylon
...		
Puzur-Sin 17th century	Liberates Aššur from foreign rule	
...		
Aššur-nadin-ahhe I 15th century		
...		

Kings of Assyria

Aššur-uballiṭ I 1356–1322	First king of Assyria	Royal Scribe Marduk-nadin-ahhe
...		

Adad-nerari I 1300–1270		
Shalmaneser I 1269–1241	Final defeat of Mittani	Ibašši-ili, first viceroy of Hanigalbat
Tukulti-Ninurta I 1240–1205	Capture of Babylon	
...		
Aššur-nerari III 1200–1195	Succession crisis	Ili-pada, last viceroy of Hanigalbat
...		
Ninurta-apil-Ekur 1189–1178		
...		
Tiglath-pileser I 1114–1076	Famine starts causing migrations	
...		
Aššur-bel-kala 1073–1056		
...		
Aššur-dan II 935–912	Conquest of lost territories begins	
Adad-nerari II 911–891		
Tukulti-Ninurta II 890–884		
Aššurnasirpal II 883–859	879: New capital Kalhu	Master Scholar Gabbu-ilani-ereš, Palace Overseer Nergal-apil-kumu'a
Shalmaneser III 858–824	Ancient borders restored	
Šamši-Adad V 823–811		
Adad-nerari III 810–783		Governor Nergal-ereš
...		
Tiglath-pileser III 744–727	Conquest of new territories begins	

Shalmaneser V 726–722		
Sargon II 721–705	706: New capital Dur-Šarrukin	Ambassador Aššur-reṣuwa
Sennacherib 704–681	c.700: New capital Nineveh	Hezekiah, king of Judah
Esarhaddon 680–669	672: Covenant with all subjects	680–612: People of Chapter 3
Aššurbanipal 668–630		Šamaš-šumu-ukin, king of Babylon
Aššur-etel-ilani 629–627		
Sin-šarru-iškun 626–612	614: Destruction of Aššur temple	Nabopolassar, king of Babylon
Aššur-uballiṭ II 611–608	612: Fall of Nineveh	

Rulers of Aššur

Cyrus II of Persia 538–530	Second Aššur temple ('Temple A')	Assyrian community in Uruk
…		
R'uth-Assor 1st century AD	Third Aššur temple ('Parthian')	Church of the East
…	c. 240: Destruction of Aššur temple	Ardashir I, king of Sassanian Empire
		Saint Matthew and Saint Behnam

References

Chapter 1: Introducing Assyria

Irving Finkel, ed., *The Cyrus Cylinder: The King of Persia's Proclamation from Ancient Babylon* (London & New York: I.B. Tauris, 2013).

Mario Liverani, 'From city-state to empire: the case of Assyria', in *The Roman Empire in Context: Historical and Comparative Perspectives*, ed. Johann P. Arnason and Kurt A. Raaflaub, 251–69 (Oxford: Wiley-Blackwell, 2011).

Mirko Novák and Helen Younansardaroud, 'Mar Behnam, Sohn des Sanherib von Nimrud: Tradition und Rezeption assyrischer Gestalten im iraqischen Christentum und die Frage nach dem Fortleben der Assyrer', *Altorientalische Forschungen*, 29 (2002): 166–94.

Diana Pickworth, 'Excavations at Nineveh: the Halzi Gate', *Iraq*, 67 (2005): 295–316.

Chapter 2: Assyrian places

Aššur

Pauline O. Harper, Evelyn Klengel-Brandt, Joan Aruz, and Kim Benzel, eds., *Assyrian Origins: Discoveries at Ashur on the Tigris* (New York: Metropolitan Museum of Art, 1995).

Stefan M. Maul, 'Die tägliche Speisung des Assur (*ginā'u*) und deren politische Bedeutung', in *Time and History in the Ancient Near East*, ed. Luis Feliu, Jaume Llop, Adelina Millet Alba, and Joaquín Sanmartín, 561–74 (Winona Lake IN: Eisenbrauns, 2013).

Nicholas Postgate, *Bronze Age Bureaucracy: Writing and the Practice of Government in Assyria* (Cambridge: Cambridge University Press, 2014): chapter 4.

Kaneš

Gojko Barjamovic, Thomas Hertel, and Mogens Trolle Larsen, *Ups and downs at Kanesh: Chronology, History and Society in the Old Assyrian Period* (Leiden: Nederlands Instituut voor het Nabije Oosten, 2012).

Tahsin Özgüç, *Kültepe Kaniš-Neša: The Earliest International Trade Center and the Oldest Capital City of the Hittites* (Istanbul: Middle Eastern Culture Center in Japan, 2003).

Sharon R. Steadman and Gregory McMahon, eds., *The Oxford Handbook of Ancient Anatolia* (Oxford & New York: Oxford University Press, 2011): chapter 13 (Cécile Michel), chapter 47 (Fikri Kulakoğlu).

Kalhu

John E. Curtis, Henrietta McCall, Dominique Collon, and Lamia al-Gailani-Werr, eds., *New Light on Nimrud* (London: British Institute for the Study of Iraq, 2008)

Joan and David Oates, *Nimrud: An Assyrian Imperial City Revealed* (London: British School of Archaeology in Iraq, 2001).

Steven W. Holloway, 'Biblical Assyria and other anxieties in the British Empire', *Journal of Religion & Society*, 3 (2001): <http://moses.creighton.edu/jrs/2001/2001-12.pdf>

Dur-Katlimmu

Hartmut Kühne, 'Tell Sheikh Hamad: the Assyrian-Aramean centre of Dur-Katlimmu/Magdalu', in *100 Jahre archäologische Feldforschungen in Nordost-Syrien: eine Bilanz*, ed. Dominik Bonatz and Lutz Martin, 235–58 (Wiesbaden: Harrassowitz, 2013).

Nicholas Postgate, *Bronze Age Bureaucracy: Writing and the Practice of Government in Assyria* (Cambridge: Cambridge University Press, 2014): chapter 5.5.

Frans A. M. Wiggermann, 'The seal of Ili-pada, Grand Vizier of the Middle Assyrian Empire', in *The Iconography of Cylinder Seals*, ed. Paul Taylor, 92–9 (London: Warburg Institute, 2006).

Chapter 3: Assyrians at home

Karen Radner and Heather D. Baker, eds., *The Prosopography of the Neo-Assyrian Empire* (Helsinki: Neo-Assyrian Text Corpus Project, 1998–2011).

King Esarhaddon

Mikko Luukko and Greta Van Buylaere, *The Political Correspondence of Esarhaddon* (Helsinki: Helsinki University Press, 2002): no. 59 (Sasî prophecy).

Simo Parpola, *Letters from Assyrian and Babylonian Scholars* (Helsinki: Helsinki University Press, 1993): nos. 187, 196, and 316.

Karen Radner, 'The trials of Esarhaddon: the conspiracy of 670 BC', in *Assur und sein Umland*, ed. Peter Miglus and Joaquín M. Cordoba, 165–84 (Madrid: Universidad Autónoma de Madrid, 2003).

Frances Reynolds, *The Babylonian Correspondence of Esarhaddon* (Helsinki: Helsinki University Press, 2003): no. 100 (Urdu-Mullissi's conspiracy).

Ivan Starr, *Queries to the Sungod: Divination and Politics in Sargonid Assyria* (Helsinki: Helsinki University Press, 1990): no. 139.

Scholars

Mikko Luukko and Greta Van Buylaere, *The Political Correspondence of Esarhaddon* (Helsinki: Helsinki University Press, 2002): nos. 34 and 35.

Simo Parpola, *Letters from Assyrian and Babylonian Scholars* (Helsinki: Helsinki University Press, 1993): no. 294.

Karen Radner, 'The Assyrian king and his scholars: the Syro-Anatolian and the Egyptian schools', *Studia Orientalia*, 106 (2009): 221–38.

Landowner

Karen Radner, *Die neuassyrischen Texte aus Tall Šēḫ Ḥamad* (Berlin: Reimer, 2002).

Wine merchant

Peter Miglus, Karen Radner, and Franciszek M. Stępniowski, *Untersuchungen im Stadtgebiet von Assur: Wohnquartiere in der Weststadt* (Wiesbaden: Harrassowitz, forthcoming).

Chapter 4: Assyrians abroad

Family matters

Cécile Michel, 'The private archives from Kaniš belonging to Anatolians', *Altorientalische Forschungen*, 38 (2011): 94–115.

Cécile Michel, 'Akkadian texts: women in letters – Old Assyrian Kaniš', in *Women in the Ancient Near East*, ed. Mark W. Chavalas, 205–12 (London & New York: Routledge, 2013).

Envoys

William L. Moran, *The Amarna Letters* (Baltimore & London: Johns Hopkins University Press, 1992): nos. 15 and 16.

Amanda H. Podany, *Brotherhood of Kings: How International Relations Shaped the Ancient Near East* (New York & Oxford: Oxford University Press, 2010).

Nicholas Postgate, *Bronze Age Bureaucracy: Writing and the Practice of Government in Assyria* (Cambridge: Cambridge University Press, 2014): chapter 5.3.

Banished to the mountains

Albert Kirk Grayson, *Assyrian Rulers of the Early First Millennium BC*, vol. 1 (Toronto: University of Toronto Press, 1991): inscriptions of Aššur-bel-kala, Aššur-dan II and Aššurnasirpal II.

Wiebke Kirleis and Michael Herles, 'Climate change as a reason for Assyro-Aramaean conflicts? Pollen evidence for drought at the end of the 2nd millennium BC', *State Archives of Assyria Bulletin*, 16 (2007): 7–37.

Jehuda Neumann and Simo Parpola, 'Climatic change and the eleventh-tenth-century eclipse of Assyria and Babylonia', *Journal of Near Eastern Studies*, 46 (1987): 161–82 (translation of 1082 BC chronicle text: p. 178).

Karen Radner, *Das mittelassyrische Tontafelarchiv von Giricano/ Dunnu-ša-Uzibi* (Turnhout: Brepols, 2004).

Unpopular ambassador

Giovanni B. Lanfranchi and S. Parpola, *The Correspondence of Sargon II, Part II: Letters from the Northern and Northeastern Provinces* (Helsinki: Helsinki University Press, 1990): chapter 6.

Simo Parpola, *The Correspondence of Sargon II*, Part I: *Letters from Assyria and the West* (Helsinki: Helsinki University Press, 1987): no. 29 (kidnapping plot).

Simo Parpola and K. Watanabe, *Neo-Assyrian Treaties and Loyalty Oaths* (Helsinki: Helsinki University Press, 1988): no. 5 (treaty with Tyre).

Karen Radner, 'Between a rock and a hard place: Musasir, Kumme, Ukku and Šubria – the buffer states between Assyria and Urartu', in *Biainili-Urartu*, ed. Stefan Kroll et al., 243–64 (Leuven: Peeters, 2012).

Sibling rivalry

Frederick Mario Fales, 'After Ta'yinat: the new status of Esarhaddon's *adê* for Assyrian political history', *Revue d'Assyriologie*, 106 (2012): 133–58.

Grant Frame, 'Šamaš-šuma-ukīn', in *Reallexikon der Assyriologie und Vorderasiatischen Archäologie*, 11, ed. Michael P. Streck et al., 618–21 (Berlin & New York: de Gruyter, 2006–8).

Richard C. Steiner, 'The Aramaic text in demotic script', in *Context of Scripture 1: Canonical Compositions from the Biblical World*, ed. W. W. Hallo, 309–27 (Leiden & Boston: Brill, 1997).

Chapter 5: Foreigners in Assyria

Role model

Hannes Galter, 'Textanalyse assyrischer Königsinschriften: der Aufstand des Puzur-Sin', *State Archives of Assyria Bulletin*, 14 (2002–5): 1–21.

Albert Kirk Grayson, *Assyrian Rulers of the Third and Second Millennia BC* (Toronto: University of Toronto Press, 1987): inscriptions of Šamši-Adad and Puzur-Sin.

Erle Leichty, *The Royal Inscriptions of Esarhaddon, King of Assyria (680–669 BC)* (Winona Lake IN: Eisenbrauns, 2011).

Regine Pruzsinszky, *Mesopotamian Chronology of the 2nd Millennium BC: An Introduction to the Textual Evidence and Related Chronological Issues* (Vienna: Verlag der Österreichischen Akademie der Wissenschaften, 2009): chapter 9.

Nele Ziegler, 'Šamšī-Adad I.', in *Reallexikon der Assyriologie und Vorderasiatischen Archäologie*, 11, ed. Michael P. Streck et al., 632–5 (Berlin & New York: de Gruyter, 2006–8).

Royal Scribe

Frans A. M. Wiggermann, 'A Babylonian scholar in Assur', in *Studies in Ancient Near Eastern World View and Society Presented to*

Marten Stol, ed. R. J. van der Spek, 203–34 (Bethesda MA: CDL Press, 2008).

Royal hostages

Albert Kirk Grayson, *Assyrian Rulers of the Early First Millennium BC*, vol. 1 (Toronto: University of Toronto Press, 1991): inscription of Tiglath-pileser I.

Karen Radner, 'After Eltekeh: royal hostages from Egypt at the Assyrian court', in *Stories of Long Ago: Festschrift für Michael D. Roaf*, ed. Heather D. Baker, Kai Kaniuth, and Adelheid Otto, 471–9 (Münster: Ugarit Verlag, 2012).

Iranian family

Kaisa Åkerman, 'The "Aussenhaken Area" in the city of Assur during the second half of the 7th century BC', *State Archives of Assyria Bulletin*, 13 (1999–2001): 217–72.

Andreas Fuchs and Simo Parpola, *The Correspondence of Sargon II, Part III: Letters from Babylonia and the Eastern Provinces* (Helsinki: Helsinki University Press, 2001): chapter 4.

Karen Radner, 'Assyria and the Medes', in *The Oxford Handbook of Ancient Iran*, ed. Daniel T. Potts, 442–56 (Oxford & New York: Oxford University Press, 2013).

Prisoners of war

Betina Faist, 'An Elamite deportee', in *Homeland and Exile: Biblical and Ancient Near Eastern Studies in Honour of Bustenay Oded*, ed. G. Galil et al., 59–69 (Leiden & Boston: Brill, 2009).

Chapter 6: Assyrian world domination: pathfinder empire

Army

Robin Archer, 'Chariotry to cavalry: developments in the early first millennium', in *New Perspectives on Ancient Warfare*, ed. Garrett G. Fagan and Matthew Trundle, 57–80 (Leiden & Boston: Brill, 2010).

Andreas Fuchs, 'Assyria at war: strategy and conduct', in *The Oxford Handbook of Cuneiform Culture*, ed. Karen Radner and Eleanor Robson, 380–401 (Oxford: Oxford University Press, 2011).

Mario Liverani, 'Assyria in the ninth century: continuity or change?', in *From the Upper Sea to the Lower Sea: Studies on the History of*

Assyria and Babylonia in Honour of A. K. Grayson, ed. Grant Frame and Linda S. Wilding, 213–26 (Leiden: Nederlands Instituut voor het Nabije Oosten, 2004).

Absolute monarchy

Dominique Collon, *Catalogue of the Western Asiatic Seals in the British Museum, Cylinder Seals 5: Neo-Assyrian and Neo-Babylonian Periods* (London: British Museum Press, 2001): no. 151.

Stephen Lumsden, 'Narrative art and empire: the throneroom of Aššurnasirpal II', in *Assyria and Beyond: Studies Presented to Mogens Trolle Larsen*, ed. Jan Gerrit Dercksen, 359–85 (Leiden: Nederlands Instituut voor het Nabije Oosten, 2004).

John Nicholas Postgate, 'The land of Assur and the yoke of Assur', *World Archaeology*, 23 (1992): 247–63.

Karen Radner, 'Assyrian and non-Assyrian kingship in the first millennium BC', in *Concepts of Kingship in Antiquity*, ed. Giovanni B. Lanfranchi and Robert Rollinger, 15–24 (Padova: Sargon srl, 2010).

Michael Roaf, 'The décor of the throne room of the palace of Ashurnasirpal', in *New Light on Nimrud*, ed. John E. Curtis, Henrietta McCall, Dominique Collon, and Lamia al-Gailani-Werr, 209–14 (London: British School of Archaeology in Iraq, 2008).

Long-distance communication

Karen Radner, 'An imperial communication network: the state correspondence of the Neo-Assyrian Empire', in *State Correspondence in the Ancient World: From New Kingdom Egypt to the Roman Empire*, ed. Karen Radner, 64–93 (New York & Oxford: Oxford University Press, 2014).

Resettlement programme

Mikko Luukko, *The Correspondence of Tiglath-pileser III and Sargon II from Calah/Nimrud* (Helsinki: Neo-Assyrian Text Corpus Project, 2012): nos. 17 and 18.

Peter Machinist, 'Assyrians on Assyria in the first millennium BC', in *Anfänge politischen Denkens in der Antike: die nahöstlichen Kulturen und die Griechen*, ed. Kurt Raaflaub, 77–104 (Munich: Oldenbourg, 1993).

Bustenay Oded, *Mass Deportations and Deportees in the Neo-Assyrian Empire* (Wiesbaden: Harrassowitz, 1979).

Aššurbanipal's Library

Grant Frame and Andrew R. George, 'The royal libraries of Nineveh: new evidence for King Ashurbanipal's tablet collection', *Iraq*, 67 (2005): 265–84.

Eleanor Robson, 'Reading the libraries of Assyria and Babylonia', in *Ancient Libraries*, ed. Jason König, Katerina Oikonomopoulou and Greg Woolf, 38–56. (Cambridge: Cambridge University Press, 2013).

Ursula Seidl, 'Assurbanipals Griffel', *Zeitschrift für Assyriologie und Vorderasiatische Archäologie*, 97 (2007): 119–24.

Further reading

Hartmut Kühne, 'State and empire of Assyria in northeast Syria', in *Archéologie et Histoire de la Syrie 1: La Syrie de l'époque néolithique à l'âge du fer*, ed. Winfried Orthmann, Paolo Matthiae, and Michel al-Maqdissi, 473–98 (Wiesbaden: Harrassowitz, 2013).

Amélie Kuhrt, *The Ancient Near East, c. 3000–330 BC* (London & New York: Routledge, 1995).

Joachim Marzahn and Beate Salje, eds., *Wiedererstehendes Assur: 100 Jahre deutsche Ausgrabungen in Assyrien* (Mainz: Zabern, 2003).

Karen Radner and Eleanor Robson, eds., *The Oxford Handbook of Cuneiform Culture* (Oxford: Oxford University Press, 2011).

Johannes Renger, ed., *Assur—Gott, Stadt und Land* (Wiesbaden: Harrassowitz, 2011).

Second millennium BC

Brian Brown, 'The structure and decline of the Middle Assyrian state: the role of autonomous and nonstate actors', *Journal of Cuneiform Studies*, 65 (2013): 97–126.

Jan Gerrit Dercksen, *Old Assyrian Institutions* (Leiden: Nederlands Instituut voor het Nabije Oosten, 2004).

Jan Gerrit Dercksen, ed., *Anatolia and the Jazira during the Old Assyrian Period* (Leiden: Nederlands Instituut voor het Nabije Oosten, 2008).

Stefan Jakob, *Mittelassyrische Verwaltung und Sozialstruktur: Untersuchungen* (Leiden & Boston: Brill, 2003).

Mario Liverani, *The Ancient Near East: History, Society and Economy* (London & New York: Routledge, 2014): chapters 12, 20, 27.

Aline Tenu, *L'expansion médio-assyrienne: approche archéologique* (Oxford: Oxbow, 2009).

Klaas R. Veenhof and Jesper Eidem, *Mesopotamia: The Old Assyrian Period* (Fribourg: Academic Press; Göttingen: Vandenhoeck & Ruprecht, 2008).

First millennium BC

Joan Aruz, Sarah B. Graff, and Yelena Rakic, eds., *Assyria to Iberia at the Dawn of the Classical Age* (New York: Metropolitan Museum of Art, 2014).

Hermann Born and Ursula Seidl, *Schutzwaffen aus Assyrien und Urartu* (Mainz: Zabern, 1995).

Ada Cohen and Steven E. Kangas, eds., *Assyrian Reliefs from the Palace of Ashurnasirpal II: A Cultural Biography* (Hanover & London: University Press of New England, 2010).

Paul Collins, *Assyrian Palace Sculptures* (London: British Museum Press, 2008).

John E. Curtis and Julian E. Reade, eds., *Art and Empire: Treasures from Assyria in the British Museum* (New York: Metropolitan Museum of Art, 1995).

David Damrosch, *The Buried Book: The Loss and Rediscovery of the Great Epic of Gilgamesh* (New York: Holt, 2007).

Tamás Dezső, *The Assyrian Army 1: The Structure of the Neo-Assyrian Army* (Budapest: Eötvös University Press, 2012).

Frederick Mario Fales, *Guerre et paix en Assyrie: religion et impérialisme* (Paris: Cerf, 2010).

Albert Kirk Grayson, *Assyrian Rulers of the Early First Millennium BC*, vol. 2 (Toronto: University of Toronto Press, 1996).

Isaac Kalimi and Seth Richardson, ed., *Sennacherib at the Gates of Jerusalem: Story, History and Historiography* (Leiden & Boston: Brill, 2014).

Mogens Trolle Larsen, *The Conquest of Assyria: Excavations in an Antique Land* (London & New York: Routledge, 1996).

Mario Liverani, *The Ancient Near East: History, Society and Economy* (London & New York: Routledge, 2014): chapters 28–31.

Stefan M. Maul, *Die Wahrsagekunst im Alten Orient: Zeichen des Himmels und der Erde* (Munich: Beck, 2013).

Simo Parpola and Robert Whiting, eds., *Assyria 1995* (Helsinki: Neo-Assyrian Text Corpus Project, 1997).

Karen Radner, 'The Neo-Assyrian Empire', in *Imperien und Reiche in der Weltgeschichte: Epochenübergreifende und globalhistorische Vergleiche*, ed. Michael Gehler and Robert Rollinger, 101–20 (Wiesbaden: Harrassowitz, 2014).

John Malcolm Russell, *Sennacherib's Palace Without Rival at Nineveh* (Chicago & London: University of Chicago Press, 1991).

John Malcolm Russell, *From Nineveh to New York: The Strange Story of the Assyrian Reliefs in the Metropolitan Museum and the Hidden Masterpiece at Cranford School* (New Haven & London: Yale University Press, 1997).

John Malcolm Russell, *The Writing on the Wall: Studies in the Architectural Context of Late Assyrian Palace Inscriptions* (Winona Lake IN: Eisenbrauns, 1999).

Irene J. Winter, *On Art in the Ancient Near East*, Volume I: *Of the First Millennium B.C.E.* (Leiden & Boston, Brill, 2010).

Websites

Assyrian Empire Builders: <http://www.ucl.ac.uk/sargon/>

Excavations at Tell Shech Hamad: <http://www.schechhamad.de>

Knowledge and Power in the Neo-Assyrian Empire: <http://oracc.museum.upenn.edu/saao/knpp/>

Kuyunjik Collection of the British Museum: <http://cdli.ucla.edu/collections/bm/bm.html>

Livius: Mesopotamia: <http://www.livius.org/babylonia.html>

Nimrud: Materialities of Assyrian Knowledge Production: <http://oracc.museum.upenn.edu/nimrud>

Royal Inscriptions of the Neo-Assyrian Period: <http://oracc.museum.upenn.edu/rinap>

State Archives of Assyria Online: <http://oracc.museum.upenn.edu/saao>

Index

Expand your collection of
VERY SHORT INTRODUCTIONS